LYNDON B. JOHNSON

A biography by Harry Provence

Harry Provence, a Texas newspaper editor, has personally known Lyndon Johnson since he was first elected to Congress more than thirty years ago. From this close association and long-time observation, he has succeeded in creating a vivid picture of Lyndon B. Johnson—the politician and the man.

LYNDON B. JOHNSON

A Biography by Harry Provence

PAPERBACK LIBRARY, Inc.
New York

PAPERBACK LIBRARY EDITION
First Printing: July, 1965

Acknowledgments

Of all the public figures ever to appear on the Texas scene, Lyndon B. Johnson has been the most fascinating to observe. Every reporter and journalist who has had the opportunity has written about him. Political observers such as Sam Wood of Austin and Waco, Allen Duckworth of Austin and Dallas, Sam Kinch of Forth Worth and Austin, Ronnie Dugger and Willie Morris of Austin, Jim Mathis, formerly of Houston; Lorraine Barnes of Austin, Booth Mooney of Washington, have enriched the written record of Johnson the politician and Johnson the man. To them, and to many others, any biographer of Lyndon B. Johnson is indebted for helping to capture some of the facets of this many-sided leader.

It would be impossible to list all the other persons who have contributed in one or another way to this account of the man who is now president of the United States. There is a special place reserved for those who have served on his staff: Mary Rather, Walter Jenkins, Cliff Carter, Mary Margaret Wiley Valenti, Jesse Kellam, Warren Woodward, Arthur Perty, George Lusk—their toils and loyalty on behalf of Lyndon Johnson are unsurpassed in any measure.

This Paperback Library Edition is published by arrangement with Fleet Publishing Corporation.

CONTENTS

CHAPTER I

On the sunny, windy afternoon of Thursday, November 21, 1963, Vice President and Mrs. Lyndon Baines Johnson climbed into their two-engined plane on the airstrip behind the LBJ ranch house. Their pilot taxied into takeoff position, lifted the ship into the wind, and set a course for San Antonio, sixty miles away. The Johnsons had been making arrangements to entertain President and Mrs. John F. Kennedy for the first time at the LBJ the following Saturday.

The Johnsons' plane landed at the San Antonio airport. Shortly afterward, *Air Force One,* the presidential jet, arrived from Washington. There were greetings all around as the Kennedys and their escort of Texas Congressmen debarked.

The Kennedys and the Johnsons, so different in backgrounds, had been drawn closer to each other in the ill-starred year of 1963. The Vice President stood shoulder to shoulder with Mr. Kennedy in the long series of foreign and domestic crises which had arisen on all sides. Mrs. Johnson, quietly and without fanfare, had stepped into the role of official hostess in Washington upon the bereavement and recuperation of Mrs. Kennedy following the loss of her prematurely born son.

Now, it seemed, the pressures had eased a bit. The President felt it was time to visit Texas to try to bring harmony to the faction-ridden Democratic Party, and to help the party raise funds for the 1964 campaign. He could also dedicate a new Aerospace Medical Center at San Antonio and honor Congressman Albert Thomas at Houston, have breakfast in Fort Worth, lunch in Dallas, and inspire the party faithful at a fund-raising dinner in Austin on Friday night.

The President's car led the way out of the San Antonio airport. The crowds at San Antonio enthusiastically welcomed the Kennedys and were delighted when Mrs. Kennedy joined her husband in shaking hands with many of the well-wishers. Mr. Kennedy dedicated the new medical center with a speech underlining the benefits of the space program.

The ebullient mood continued that evening at Houston, where the Kennedys and Johnsons shared the spotlight at a testimonial dinner for Congressman Thomas. The mood seemed even stronger next morning at Fort Worth, where Mr.

Kennedy addressed Cowtown citizens. He was in top form, giving a robust and good-humored catalogue of the strength of the United States.

Throughout the appearances in San Antonio, Houston and Fort Worth, Vice President Johnson stayed in the background, savoring the impact of Mr. and Mrs. Kennedy on the friendly crowds. At Houston, occasional hecklers shouted "Cuba," but it seemed to Mr. Johnson that the widely advertised Texas opposition to President Kennedy could not be so overwhelming if the thousands of cheering people were any indication.

The presidential party drove out to Carswell Air Force Base, on the edge of Fort Worth, and boarded the jet for a ten-minute hop to Dallas. This saved a thirty-five mile motor ride and put *Air Force One* in position for the scheduled flight to Austin, later.

The Mayor and other dignitaries were on hand at Dallas' Love Field to greet the Kennedys, who walked to the open limousine reserved for them. Governor and Mrs. John Connally joined them for the ride through Dallas toward the hall where the luncheon crowd was gathering. Mr. and Mrs. Johnson, with U.S. Senator Yarborough, entered another limousine. Congressmen, aides, security agents and reporters took their places in other cars.

The cavalcade moved slowly along Main Street in downtown Dallas. Crowds of men, women and children along the sidewalks waved and cheered.

In the lead car the President of the United States and his bright-eyed, smiling wife, and the graying, handsome Governor of Texas and his blonde wife, smiled back at the people. The President and his wife waved.

The big, open Secret Service car came next. In the third car, Vice President Johnson and his brunette wife, with a United States Senator beside them, attracted nearly as much attention from the crowds.

The other vehicles bearing Congressmen and reporters followed.

The President's car led the way past the end of Elm Street, down a curving concrete street leading to the freeway that would take the distinguished visitors to the huge market hall where the President was to have lunch, then make a speech calling for rejection of the doctrines of hate and fear.

As the lead car rounded the curve at the bottom of the incline, a rifle shot rang out.

At the sound and concussion of that first shot, a slim figure in the third car vaulted from the front seat to the

8

rear. Two arms pulled the startled Vice President to the floor of the back seat, and the Secret Service agent pressed his body down on the Vice President's rangy frame. Two more shots did their deadly work.

The three cars, one with the dying and wounded, another with Secret Service agents, and the third with the Vice President, sped for Parkland Hospital, nine minutes away.

In the confusion, wondering what was happening, the Vice President rode all the way to the hospital with his nose against the shoe of U.S. Senator Ralph Yarborough and with Agent Rufus Youngblood holding him to the floor.

At the hospital, the Vice President was released from his recumbent position. He helped his wife from the limousine and they walked quickly inside. The Vice President soon learned that the President was dead. Mr. Johnson leaned against a hospital corridor wall and drew deeply on the nasal inhaler he keeps at hand.

The Secret Service man in charge insisted that Mr. Johnson return at once to Washington. The implications of the murder in Dallas were unknown, the extent of the plot unguessable.

Mr. Johnson secured a swift telephone connection to Washington and the ear of the Attorney General, Robert Kennedy, brother of the slain President. "And," said the Attorney General, "you had better be sworn in as President before you start back to Washington."

Other phone calls found United States District Judge Sarah T. Hughes, and alerted the crew of *Air Force One*.

Mr. and Mrs. Johnson were driven back to the airport. In an ambulance, the plain bronze casket containing the murdered President followed. Mrs. Kennedy sat beside the casket.

At the big jet airplane, the casket was lifted aboard, and the shocked, stunned official party climbed to the cabin. Judge Hughes arrived, and went aboard. Lyndon Johnson took his stance in front of Judge Hughes. Mrs. Johnson stood at one side of him, Mrs. Kennedy at the other. Raising his left hand, and placing his right hand on the Bible, Mr. Johnson swore to perform the duties of President and to defend the Constitution of the United States. The engine noise nearly drowned out the words. The ceremony over, Judge Hughes left the plane.

The new President said, "Let's get this plane back to Washington." The pilot turned up the four jet engines and *Air Force One* was on its way.

Aboard the plane, Mrs. Kennedy kept vigil beside her husband's casket.

9

President Johnson slowly wrote out a brief and simple statement which he would make to the nation when the plane landed at Andrews Air Force Base. He dictated it to a secretary so that typed copies could be made.

Then he penned two letters, one to Caroline Kennedy, one to John Kennedy, Jr., telling them about their father's tragic death and about the loss it meant to the nation and to the world. These letters he sealed. No copies were made.

On the plane's radio telephone, he talked to the murdered President's mother in New England.

Once on the ground in Washington, President Johnson went directly to the White House, and then to the Executive Offices Building next door where his vice presidential staff awaited him.

Although he was still shocked and almost overwhelmed by the tragedy of the afternoon, President Johnson proceeded with outward calm to make the telephone calls and hold the hurried conferences necessary in this crisis. Late that night he went home to bed in his residence in northwest Washington, where the usual skeleton crew of Secret Service agents suddenly had grown to a sizable squad.

Saturday morning, President Johnson convened the Cabinet at the White House. He asked the men to stand in silence for a moment and bow their heads in tribute to the fallen leader. Afterward, he begged them to stay at their posts. The members all agreed.

Saturday was crowded with activity. Every few minutes brought news of more heads of government starting for Washington to attend President Kennedy's funeral on Monday. There was a conference with the leaders of Congress to work out plans for President Johnson to address a joint session on Wednesday, two days after the funeral.

The new President talked more than once with the head of the Central Intelligence Agency and with the head of the Department of Defense. Without announcing it, on the afternoon of the assassination, the nation's military establishment had gone on instant readiness. Expert eyes and ears assessed foreign reactions, alert for a possible signal that the slaying was meant to throw the country into turmoil and at the mercy of an enemy.

To add to the gloom, a steady, light rain began to fall.

Back and forth between the Executive Offices Building and the White House office wing went President Johnson, his presence required alternately in one place, then the other.

By nightfall Saturday, he felt that everything was done

which had to be done, and set out for his residence with a few old friends.

There, over a late dinner, they discussed the day's pressures. Mrs. Johnson, pale and somber, said little. In the midst of the quiet conversation, his younger daughter, Lucy, sixteen, walked into the breakfast room where the meal was being served. She had just received a briefing from the Secret Service. From now on, she said ruefully, her parents would be made aware of her every move.

The group moved back again into the sitting room where the television coverage of the fateful week end proceeded. On the screen came a sequence which had been filmed a few weeks previously at the Lyndon Johnson ranch in Texas.

The new President watched his own image on the screen, heard his voice say many things about the fortunate, blessed condition of the American people because of the American free enterprise system. It was a theme he liked to dwell on at any opportunity.

He looked around at his guests and said, "How do you get the people to realize that two-thirds of the other people in the world are hungry and ragged and poor? How do you make the truth of this soak in?"

A rather eloquent speaker appeared on the screen. Mr. Johnson said, "That's the way to make a speech." This reminded him of other days in Texas. Referring to well-known former Texas political figures, he said, "Somebody asked Governor Pat Neff one time how he prepared his silver-tongued speeches. He said he wrote them out and memorized every word and gesture. The fellow then went to Governor Hobby and asked him the question. Governor Hobby said he made an outline and built his speech around it. Then the fellow asked old Jim Ferguson. Old Jim said, 'I fill myself plump full of my subject, stand up and let 'er fly!'"

The talk turned to more recent events. The new President recalled a time when his advice as Vice President was sought on a legislative matter, after others involved had already agreed on a course of action. He gave a differing idea of what should be done, but only privately to the person most concerned. When the man asked him why he had not spoken out in front of the whole group, Johnson had replied, "By that time, it was too late. I would have created a scene instead of a solution."

An aide came into the room, one of the men who was working on portions of the speech which the new President would deliver to the Joint Session of Congress a few days hence.

11

Mr. Johnson arose, bade his guests good night, and went upstairs with the aide to work on into the night. He had been President of the United States for a little more than twenty-four hours.

No one can ever forget the drama piled on drama of that incredible week end. The assassination and its numbing shock . . . the floodlighted scene at Andrews when the slain President's body came off the plane and the new President, shaken, read his quiet words into the microphones . . . the scenes and sounds of Washington the next dreary day . . . the first great, majestic procession to the Capitol on Sunday . . . little John Kennedy, Jr., manfully climbing the Capitol steps, holding his mother's hand . . . the fantastic, televised shooting of the accused assassin, Lee Oswald . . . the world leaders walking behind the flag-draped casket on the cold, sunny Monday . . . the throbbing of the muffled drums . . . and the regal, veiled widow in her quiet dignity.

The miracle of television permitted the American people to participate in the historic days and nights to an extent never before imagined.

The same magic eye showed the people their new President in action as he attended to the ceremonial functions in the Capitol, the Cathedral, and at the graveside. The screen also showed him greeting the leaders of European, Asiatic, and African nations at a Department of State reception after the burial services.

But the cameras could not show him in between ceremonies, coat off most of the time, talking head to head with a series of advisers and other officials, telephoning to find persons whose voices he needed to hear. Meanwhile, in half a dozen offices nearby, a team of experts continued to work on his first major public address.

He delivered this address to a joint session of Congress on the Wednesday following the death of President Kennedy. His grasp of the national mood in the wake of the tragedy was evident in the following passage:

"John Kennedy's death commands what his life conveyed —that America must move forward. The time has come for Americans of all races and creeds and political beliefs to understand and respect one another. Let us put an end to the teaching and preaching of hate and evil and violence. Let us turn away from the fanatics of the far left and the far right, from the apostles of bitterness and bigotry, from those defiant of law, and those who pour venom into our nation's bloodstream. . . ."

12

The following evening, in his Thanksgiving message to the nation, he reaffirmed this message:

"In each administration, the greatest burden that the President has had to bear has been the burden of his own countrymen's unthinking and unreasoning hate and division. So, in these days, the fate of this office is the fate of us all. I would ask all Americans on this day of prayer and reverence to think on these things. Let all who speak and all who teach and all who preach and all who publish and all who broadcast and all who read or listen—let them reflect upon their responsibilities to bind our wounds, to heal our sores, to make our society well and whole for the tasks ahead of us. It is this work that I most wanted us to do, to banish rancor from our words and malice from our hearts, to close down the poison spring of hatred and intolerance and fanaticism; to protect our unity north and south, east and west; to hasten the day when bias of race, religion and region is no more; and to make the day when our great energies and decencies and spirit will be free of the burdens we have borne too long. . . ."

It was not merely the shocking death of the young President that brought from Lyndon Johnson these exhortations. He had lived through the period when "Roosevelt-hater" became a part of the language. He had witnessed the bitterness directed at Harry Truman. He had heard the opprobrium heaped on Dwight D. Eisenhower's head by critics of the far left and far right. And Lyndon Johnson himself had been reviled, spat upon, and made the target of contempt and ridicule time without number in the thirty-two years of his public career.

At close range he had studied the presidency and its potential and uses through the administration of Herbert Hoover, Franklin D. Roosevelt, Harry Truman, Dwight Eisenhower and John F. Kennedy. His intimate acquaintance with the latter four Presidents, based on his own rising position in the Congress, taught him the pitfalls, the opportunities, and the difficulties of the presidency.

Even so, he was somewhat shaken on the first morning as President, when, as he told friends later that day, aides came to brief him on twenty major controversial domestic problems, all of which had been bucked along the line to the President's desk, not one with a recommended solution. They ranged from the bitter railroad labor dispute to the question of price supports on American rice crops.

13

Mr. Johnson had no ready solutions, but he did not flinch from the task of finding them.

This instinct for going out to meet a situation, coupled with his rich experience in politics and government, engendered in all quarters of the nation, regardless of party affiliations, a sense of gratitude that Lyndon Johnson was leading the country in this tragic aftermath.

CHAPTER II

Politics in the ancestry of Lyndon Baines Johnson goes as far back as his family history can be traced: to Scottish parliamentarians through his maternal grandmother's line; to early American officeholders on both sides of the family tree.

Equally strong in his heritage is the tradition of school-teaching. And the Johnsons, of course, pioneered as farmers in the old South and as cattlemen in the hills of Texas.

The lure of Texas as a land of plenty and a cradle of new civilization pulled both sides of Lyndon Johnson's antecedents to the state years before the Civil War. The Johnsons came for land and grass. The Rev. George Washington Baines came to propagate the Christian faith through the Baptist denomination. Each moved westward in the traditional search for better tomorrows.

Jesse Johnson and Lucy Webb Barnett Johnson lived in Georgia as a farm couple long enough to raise nine children, then moved on to Alabama in the 1830's. Their tenth child, Samuel Ealy Johnson, was born in that period. Then Texas drew the Jesse Johnsons to a settlement called Lockhart, in the south central region in 1856. Tom Johnson and Sam Ealy Johnson headed the family enterprise of ranging cattle in the rugged hills and fertile valleys of Gillespie County. They especially liked a wide portion of the valley of the winding, shallow Pedernales River in the eastern edge of the county because of its added expanse of grazing land and its sheltered isolation.

Even before the Civil War, the Texas hill country had become a starting point for occasional cattle drives to Missouri where beef brought better prices. The Johnsons drove herds of steers northward, came out well in the process, and seemed started on the road to prosperity. Secession and war intervened.

On September 18, 1861, Sam Ealy Johnson went back to Lockhart to enlist in De Bray's Regiment of the Confederate States Army. He served forty-eight months unscathed, though his horse was shot dead under him in the battle of Pleasant Hill on April 9, 1864.

Back from the war, Sam Johnson found turbulent conditions in Blanco County. War-shattered Texas couldn't protect its frontiers. The Lipan and Commanche Indians raided the isolated farms and ranches in the hill country with impunity. Almost every full moon brought a marauding band on the prowl for livestock and scalps.

Sam and Tom Johnson built their stone barn as a fort with gun slits. They and their kin built stone cabins clustered around the fort. They resumed the business of buying and trailing cattle to the northern markets, taking a full part in the great wave of trail-driving that brought prostrate Texas its first hard money in the aftermath of war.

The Johnson ranch headquarters with its sturdy fort became a rallying point for other settlers as Indian troubles continued. It also became a bridal suite for Samuel Ealy Johnson and Eliza Bunton when they married in 1867.

Black-haired, sharp-eyed Eliza Bunton was a niece of John Wheeler Bunton, a signer of the Declaration of Independence of the Republic of Texas in 1836 and of its constitution, as well as a member of its first Congress. One of her cousins was a cofounder of the Daughters of the American Revolution. An uncle was a governor of Kentucky. Her Scottish forebears had been members of Parliament for generations.

Eliza Bunton Johnson was brave enough to stay at the Johnson ranch undaunted while the men went off for months on end to drive cattle to Kansas. Several times she saw horses dashing madly home from Indian fights, arrows sticking from their flanks. Once she hid beneath a cabin floor as Indians ransacked the premises.

The archives show that Samuel Johnson came out luckier than most of his neighbors, if he reported all his Indian losses. The official documents list him only once, as having suffered theft of a saddle horse worth $50. Other Blanco County settlers lost tens, scores, hundreds of head of horses, mules and cattle to the Indians—more than several thousand animals in nine years.

But the country finally settled down after the last Indian fight a few miles from the Johnson ranch in 1873. By this time so many families were living in the vicinity that the entire settlement was called Johnson City. The name seems to have started as a sort of joke among the Johnson clan, but it stuck. Ninety years later, in 1960, Johnson City had grown to 611 souls.

In 1877, Samuel and Eliza Johnson welcomed the birth of their son, and they gave him his father's name.

The cattle trail drives in Texas ended with the coming of barbed wire, and the hill country of Texas became a rather isolated backwater. All the available farm land in the valleys had been settled early. The hills missed the population boom

16

that brought hundreds of thousands of families to Texas in the 1870's and 1880's when barbed wire and windmills made prairie farming possible.

In the valley of the Pedernales, crops and animals were sufficient to make a living, but money stayed scarce.

The other side of the family that ultimately produced Lyndon Baines Johnson can be traced back to colonial America. One ancestor, Thomas Jameson, was in Braddock's army in the French and Indian War, and later stood near George Washington at Yorktown when General Cornwallis surrendered. The line that eventually came to Texas began in Ireland, from which a Baptist preacher, the Rev. George Bains, emigrated to North Carolina. His son, Thomas, became a farmer. It was he who Anglicized the family name, inserting an "e" to spell it "Baines." Thomas Baines's eldest son, born December 30, 1809, near Raleigh, North Carolina, was George Washington Baines.

Thomas Baines took his family to Georgia, and then to Alabama, where George Washington Baines grew up on the farm without formal education. An old chronicle says:

". . . After he became of age, by his own unaided efforts, first by cutting and rafting timber and afterwards by teaching school, he nearly finished the full course of study at the University of Alabama. His health failing (he was a lifelong dyspeptic), he left school during his senior year in 1836. . . ."

The young schoolteacher attended a revival meeting during his college days, was converted to Christianity as a Baptist, and by the time he left the university was licensed to preach. In quest of a healthier climate, he traveled to the wilderness of northern Arkansas, where he built a log cabin, mustered the settlers for church worship, and was elected to the state legislature. He also won a reputation as a hunter: "Whether the hunt was for turkey, deer, or bear, he seldom returned empty-handed. The pioneers liked this in their preacher. . . ."

George Washington Baines married Melissa Ann Butler in 1840 in Carroll County, Arkansas: "Their bridal tour was from her father's house to her husband's new cabin, and she rode behind him on the same horse. Nine children were born to them; four survived. . . ."

The sharpshooting frontier minister heard a call of duty to Louisiana in 1844. He became acknowledged as the foremost preacher of the northern part of that state. He also served as president of a college at Mount Pleasant and was superintendent of schools for Bienville Parish for a time. Then ". . . he visited Texas, assisted in the organization of a

Baptist church at Marshall. He caught the Texas fever. . . ." This old expression referred to a common syndrome of those days, the desire to settle in that new and promising part of the country.

In 1850, the Rev. George Washington Baines and his family, including his son Joseph Wilson Baines, moved to Huntsville, Texas. Here the Baptist flock flourished; and its members, including General Sam Houston, welcomed the Rev. Mr. Baines as pastor. A memento of that period now hangs on the office wall of Lyndon Baines Johnson. It is a letter from General Sam Houston to his pastor, dated November 23, 1857:

My Dear Brother Baines:

You will find enclosed your note, and if you will renew it for the same amount of $300 and send it to Mrs. Houston I will be obliged to you. You perceive that I knock off the interest for six years at 8 per cent per annum amounting to one hundred and forty dollars. This I am not loth to do as you have the luck to minister to Congregations who think you can afford to preach to them gratis. If you do not devise some plan to change their practice, they will think that you ought to pay them a good salary for attending church when they could stay at home on Sunday and thusly be in greater readiness for the week's work. I am not alluding to charity, tho I think the scriptures enjoin that as one of the brightest Christian traits of character, but I allude to plain old fashioned honesty of paying what they subscribe. They ought to know that paper currency will not pass in Heaven. It must be the coin which is only issued from an honest heart. Cotton fields, and cotton bolls will find no market in Paradise.

Mrs. Houston joins in affectionate regards to Sister Baines, yourself and family.

Truly Thine
Sam Houston

Rev. Mr. Baines extended his influence widely by starting and editing the first Baptist publication in Texas. Then:

". . . In 1861, when the war with all its wrecks and griefs was upon us—when stout hearts faltered and wise heads were confused, the pastor-editor laid down the work he loved so well, and yielding to the call of his brethren, accepted the presidency of Baylor University at Independence. . . ."

For two years, the Rev. Mr. Baines held this little struggling school together, before ill health caused him to resign.

18

He continued for another twenty years to be a power among Texas Baptists, and died full of honors in Bell County in 1882.

His son, Joseph Wilson Baines, after service in the army of the Confederacy, turned to the practice of law and the editing of a weekly newspaper, *The Advocate,* at McKinney in north Texas. He wrote political correspondence from that section for the Galveston *News.* And like most political writers of his day, he played an active role in the dominant Democratic Party.

The Joseph W. Baineses became parents of a daughter, Rebekah, on June 26, 1881, in McKinney.

A year later when Baines's good friend John Ireland won the governorship of Texas, Baines was appointed Secretary of State, necessitating a move to Austin, the capital. After he completed two terms, and Governor Ireland retired, J. W. Baines moved his family to Fredericksburg, thirty-one miles from Johnson City. He practiced law, continued to write for the Dallas *News,* the Galveston *News* and the San Antonio *Express,* and got himself elected to the Texas legislature for a series of terms as the representative of the Blanco-Fredericksburg district.

By then, his tall, blonde daughter Rebekah was ready for college. She attended the University of Texas for a time, Baylor University in 1901, and then went to Baylor College for Women at Belton. In her senior year, her father suffered sudden financial reverses, but she obtained a job in the college bookstore and went ahead to win her diploma.

For Samuel Ealy Johnson, Jr., growing up amidst the hard-times living on the Pedernales, the struggle to get an education seemed endless. Old Sam, Sr., had nothing but land and cattle, and neither was in demand. One year he told Sam, Jr., "Son, take this yearling. It's all I can do for your schooling this year." So Sam, Jr., butchered the animal and sold the meat from house to house in Johnson City to pay his high school expenses.

When that money was gone, young Sam took lessons from the village barber and tried his hand at barbering on Saturdays and after school. His aim was to become a school-teacher.

When it came time to take the examinations, young Sam Johnson gathered thirteen books, a sack of dried fruit to eat, and a bottle of pepsin tablets to settle his stomach, and set out for his grandmother's house to find seclusion for studying.

He passed the examinations, taught school, and later studied law. And when Joseph W. Baines retired as the local member of the legislature, young Sam Johnson stood for the position. He was elected in 1904, and sat for the first time in the session of 1905.

Joseph W. Baines and his daughter were living in Austin then, where Mr. Baines wrote political news, practiced law and dabbled in politics. He kept a fatherly eye on the young man who had succeeded him in the legislature. Rebekah Baines helped her father in his newspaper reporting. She preferred politics to any other field of interest.

One day in 1906, J. W. Baines asked Rebekah to interview young Representative Sam Johnson on some currently lively political question.

It was the first meeting of Sam Johnson and Rebekah Baines. She liked to tell about it in later years:

"I asked him lots of questions but he was pretty cagey and I couldn't pin him down. I was awfully provoked with that man!"

Never before had Sam Johnson met a pretty and vivacious girl whose interest was politics. He began to seek her out. Their courtship consisted of attending political meetings, Confederate Veterans reunions, and other affairs where politics furnished the central theme. Then they quit talking politics and Sam Johnson won her promise to marry him.

The wedding took place at Fredericksburg on August 20, 1907.

The young couple set up their household in a frame cottage on the banks of the Pedernales River sixteen miles west of Johnson City. For a family history, Mrs. Johnson wrote this comment on her husband's farming talent:

"He was a natural farmer. He improved the house, set out the orchard, tended the vegetable garden. . . ."

And in that cottage, one year and one week after their wedding day, Rebekah Johnson gave birth to her first son, August 27, 1908.

Nobody was more excited than his grandfather, Sam Johnson, the old trail driver. He mounted his horse that Sunday afternoon, so the family scrapbook reports, and rode around to all the neighbors and relatives to announce, "A United States Senator was born today . . . my grandson."

The baby boy remained nameless for three months. Sam and Rebekah could not agree on a first name. Mr. Johnson liked the names Clarence and Dayton, but his wife firmly refused both. Finally, Sam Johnson proposed the boy be called Linden, after an old friend of the family. Mrs. Johnson said it sounded all right, but it would look better if it were spelled Lyndon. Thus Lyndon Baines Johnson finally acquired his first identity.

CHAPTER III

Life on the Pedernales a half-century ago was meager for Sam and Rebekah Johnson. The harvest of grain and livestock off the small farm brought a modest cash return. Sam Johnson's salary as a member of the legislature was welcome when he received it, but the $5 a day came only every other year and then only for the period of the session itself, one hundred and twenty days.

In the frame house beneath the spreading oak trees overlooking the stream, Mrs. Johnson cared for her infant son. To do the laundry required water drawn from the well, heated over a wood fire, strong, home-made soap and plenty of hard scrubbing. To cook their meals required more firewood for the kitchen stove. It was a life of never-ending chores and toil. At night, kerosene lamps illuminated the plainly furnished rooms.

There were neighbors living along the Johnsons' side of the Pedernales—relatives of Sam Johnson, and friends. Life may have been hard but it wasn't lonely. The families of the vicinity enjoyed each other's company and shared each other's problems.

Sam Johnson acknowledged this every time he returned home from a legislative session in Austin, seventy miles away. "I'm glad to get back home in the hills," he said. "Here's where they know when you're sick, and they care when you die."

As a child, Lyndon enjoyed playing with the neighborhood youngsters. And he enjoyed learning from his mother, she often said later. By using a set of lettered blocks, she taught him the alphabet by the time he was three years old. It was then, too, that he began to follow his older playmates to school. The teacher allowed him to sit in the classroom, and when he showed interest in the lessons, she began teaching him the work of the first grade in its simplest form.

The chief difference between him and the other first graders appeared when she asked Lyndon to read aloud. He insisted on sitting in the teacher's lap because that was the way he read for his mother at home.

Two other babies, Rebekah and Josefa, were born to Mrs. Johnson during those years on the farm. When the Sam Johnsons moved to Johnson City in 1913, Sam Houston

Johnson arrived as their fourth child, and a year or two later Lucia, the last of the children, was born.

Lyndon was five when the family moved into town. Their home was a rambling white frame house set on the north side of a block-sized lot, with well and water tank and out-buildings in the rear. Sam Johnson traded in real estate and cattle and had a small interest in the local bank, but he made hardly more than a living.

He was, however, a ranking member of "The Establishment" of Blanco County, the people who pretty much decided who would run for public office and led in electing their choices. Sam Johnson was a warm and friendly man. He held many a political conversation on the front porch of the house in Johnson City, and quite often his growing son Lyndon was in the bedroom adjoining the porch, listening through the window to the way things went in local politics.

Lyndon Johnson remembers one morning in particular, he says, when a friend came to talk to his father on the porch, bringing word that it appeared as though seventy close-knit German family votes in a nearby valley were going over to the other side in the next election. Sam Johnson, calm as always, told the friend to visit the head of this German clan and say that, on account of the incumbent county judge's ill health, folks were thinking that this worthy German would be the logical man to become county judge before long.

Next day, Sam Johnson's friend came to report results. "I went out to the farm and found old man —— sitting on a zinc bucket, milking his cow into another bucket. His wife was up in the loft throwing hay down for the cattle. I told him what you said, Sam, and he came up off that bucket like it was hot. And she nearly fell out of the loft." When the votes were counted, the seventy ballots in that valley were on Sam Johnson's side.

Lyndon Johnson never tires of talking about political lessons he learned from his father. "He used to say that if you couldn't come into a roomful of people and tell right away who was for you and who was against you, you had no business in politics," says the son. He has kept for years on an office wall a saying of his father: "When you're talking, you ain't learnin' nothin'."

Sam Johnson had a special way of making his gangling son get up in the mornings, too. He'd shake him and say, "Get up, son, every other boy in the county is two hours ahead of you."

But life for young Lyndon Johnson included more work

than listening. During World War I, he shined shoes in the barbershop at Johnson City. It was a way to pick up spending money, the scarcest commodity in town. He worked as a printer's devil at the weekly newspaper office. He herded goats on nearby ranches.

In between the chores and the schooling, Lyndon and his young friends roamed the countryside near Johnson City, sometimes on foot, sometimes on horses. They swam in a deep natural pool on the Pedernales during the warm months. If the girls insisted on swimming, too, the boys wore bathing suits.

Oldtimers around Johnson City remember that the boy Lyndon Johnson always had time for political errands. He handed out candidates' cards and circulars. And on one memorable occasion, his father took Lyndon in a Model T Ford to a nearby town to meet the governor of Texas, who was touring the area. The governor rode with them back to Johnson City. Sam Johnson and the governor sat in the rear seat of the touring car while 12-year-old Lyndon drove them around the courthouse and all over the rest of the village so that everybody could see the governor . . . and his young chauffeur.

In the small high school, Lyndon won a place on the two-man debating team. He and his partner became county debating champions, which sent them on to compete in a district tournament. When they lost, Lyndon became physically nauseated. He wanted to win at everything he did, whether it was debating or playing dominoes.

He graduated from Johnson City High School at the age of fifteen, president of the seven-member class. He was six feet, three inches tall, skinny as a rail, big-eared, with a mop of dark hair. His imagination had grown also; he was ready to see something bigger than Johnson City.

He and five of his friends bought an automobile. Without telling anybody their plans, the six youngsters set out to drive to the fabled West Coast, where Lyndon had a relative.

They pooled their meager supply of cash, kept it in a little sack. They camped out along the road, and each night dug a hole, buried the money sack and made their blanket beds on top of it.

They reached California with no mishap, but when they started looking for work, they found that untrained hired help didn't command much of a wage.

Lyndon Johnson tried his hand at a variety of jobs—washing cars in a garage, running an elevator, washing dishes in a hash house, and picking fruit in the Imperial Valley. He admits it was a lesson in starvation. It was not difficult for his relative to persuade him to return to Johnson City.

"The prettiest sight I ever saw in my life," he said years later, "was my grandmother's patchwork quilt on the foot of my bed when I got back home." He had been sleeping either on the ground or in cheap boardinghouses.

But he still refused to think about further schooling. He got a day laborer's job on a highway work gang. He shoveled gravel, pushed a wheelbarrow, drove a tractor. He stubbornly resisted his parents' entreaties to find a way to go to college and make something out of himself.

Many of Johnson's contemporaries will understand why he felt impelled to earn a day laborer's wage instead of going to college. Little as it was, the money he held in his hand after muscle-straining toil was still money. To boys growing up in rural Texas in that decade, the sight and feel of cash money held immense satisfaction. Not for them the "Golden Twenties." That happened somewhere else, far away. Every family decision, from what to eat to whether one of the children could have a pair of shoes or a new garment, hinged on the question of whether there was money to pay for it. As often as not, the answer was "No." By staying on the road gang, he was making a tangible contribution to the family's continuing struggle against poverty. Yet his mother, with her deeper perspective and her faith in Lyndon's abilities, refused to relent in urging him to try to rise above a day laborer's horizon.

One Saturday he came home late from a night on the town that ended in a fist fight. His nose was battered and bleeding. His mother sat down beside his bed and wept unrestrainedly, lamenting his lack of ambition and his apparent indifference to her aspirations for him.

But Mrs. Johnson's arguments must have been fermenting inside her rawboned son. One cold, wet evening in February, 1927, after a grueling chore on the road gang, he came home exhausted. He greeted his mother wearily and said, "I don't know whether I can work with my brain or not, but I'm willing to try. If you and Daddy can get me into a college, I'm ready to go."

Mrs. Johnson immediately called Dr. C. E. Evans, president of Southwest State Teachers College at San Marcos, sixty miles away. Dr. Evans said, yes, bring him on to school; he could enter the preparatory work and get ready for regular enrollment.

The preparatory work had to be done because Johnson City High School was not a fully accredited institution.

24

The Johnsons scraped up a few dollars, and young Lyndon went to a bank and borrowed $75 on his personal note to start his college effort. He hitchhiked to San Marcos, went to the college, and got a job on the campus, tending shrubs and picking up rocks. He sailed into the work and into the make-up studies with equal vigor.

Mrs. Mattie Allison, head of the English Department at the San Marcos school, still remembers the new student, Lyndon Johnson. It was under her supervision that youngsters from unaccredited high schools had to prove their right to enroll full time as college students. She recalls that Lyndon Johnson from the start showed special interest in history and politics.

One day Mrs. Allison was standing in the door of her classroom when Lyndon Johnson walked up and handed her several sheets of paper. "Read this and see if you like it," he asked her.

"I hardly remember what is was, but I do recall it pertained to current politics. It was so good that I asked several members of the faculty if I were being taken in.

"I didn't really believe that a boy so young could have had such a wide grasp of politics," she says today.

In six weeks time Lyndon Johnson had made up his high school deficiencies and was enrolled as a college student in the second half of the spring semester.

Once started, he wanted to get through as soon as possible. Because he needed to earn all his school and living expenses, he obtained additional campus work, including a janitorial assignment.

Before long, he served in the office of the president as a secretary and assistant in whatever was needed. Years later, Dr. Evans liked to joke with Lyndon Johnson about his enthusiasm as assistant:

"Lyndon, I declare you hadn't been in my office a month before I could hardly tell who was president of the school—you or me."

Mrs. Allison remembers Lyndon as a fighter. The college faculty was not accustomed to a student with such initiative. "He had a peculiar effect on both the faculty and the students. You either liked him or you didn't. But Dr. Evans had the highest regard and respect for Lyndon," she said. "Lyndon as a student knew how to ingratiate himself not only with the college professors and instructors, but with his fellow students, too."

The more he did and the harder he worked at San Marcos Teachers College, the more Lyndon Johnson found to do.

Yet when his eldest sister Rebekah followed him on the college roster and the family funds wouldn't stretch to afford her the simple necessities such as lipstick and hairpins and so forth, Lyndon found another job he could perform after midnight, several times a week, stuffing and sealing envelopes. All the money he earned in that chore went to his sister for her personal needs.

Talking about this years later to a group of friends who were discussing ways of helping other people, Lyndon Johnson said, "During those years my daddy never made more than $150 a month himself, and yet all of us children got through college by helping each other. When I graduated and started teaching, I helped the younger ones. When my sister graduated and began teaching, she helped the younger ones. We all did whatever was needed."

Even with all his various jobs, young Lyndon Johnson wasn't earning enough to keep himself fed and clothed adequately, so in the summer of 1928 he followed the example of many another struggling Texas college student: he obtained a limited teaching certificate, and was given a teaching assignment. For the academic year 1928–29 Lyndon Johnson taught the fifth, sixth and seventh grades in the little town of Cotulla.

Cotulla's three thousand residents included a number of Mexican families, and Johnson's three-grade class had its share of their children. The tall, intense young teacher is still remembered for his success in prompting better feeling between the Anglo and Latin children, and for the fact that he used his first salary check at Cotulla to buy athletic equipment for the Latin boys.

Fortified by savings from his stint at Cotulla, Lyndon Johnson returned to San Marcos and college. He took up most of his old jobs, including the secretarial duties in the office of President Evans. He also won a place on the college debating team, took over the editorship of the campus newspaper, and led the non-athletic portion of the student body in a successful foray which broke up the athletes' domination of campus elections.

Through all this, he carried a full load of courses, and in the summer session of 1930, at the age of twenty-two, Lyndon Johnson received his bachelor of science degree.

In the summer of Lyndon Johnson's graduation, Texas politics waxed as hot as the summer sun. Dan Moody, fiery reform governor, was completing his second term and was leading the struggle to be sure that Mrs. Miriam A. Ferguson did not return to the office he had taken from her four years earlier. Moody spearheaded the campaign for Ross Sterling, a big, bearlike oil tycoon.

The governor's race went into a second primary runoff between Mrs. Ferguson and Ross Sterling. Also in a runoff were former governor Pat Neff, seeking an elective term as a member of the Texas Railroad Commission, and W. Gregory Hatcher, long-time state treasurer who had resigned to oppose Pat Neff.

Pat Neff had never lost a political race. He had risen by stages from city attorney at Waco to the governorship of Texas, serving in the legislature and as Speaker of the House of Representatives. He won the governorship in 1920 and was re-elected in 1924. After a hiatus of four years, he was appointed chairman of the Railroad Commission to fill an unexpired term. So in 1930 he had to face the electorate in order to stay on the commission.

Pat Neff carefully cultivated his puritan image in politics. He was a silver-tongued orator, a prime mover in the Baptist denomination and in fraternal orders. He always wore a black suit, wing collar, string tie, and his graying hair was cut long. Erect as a lodgepole, and with an eagle-beak nose, Neff never unbent, nor even donned the garb of the outdoorsman.

The Johnsons supported Mr. Neff in his Railroad Commission race.

One day there was a political rally at Henly, a crossroads village a few miles from San Marcos. Mr. and Mrs. Johnson and their newly graduated son went over to hear the orators.

There was somebody to make a speech for every candidate except Pat Neff. A man supporting Neff's opponent got up and sneered at the great Pat Neff, the man who never fired a gun nor wet a fish hook, who wouldn't know what to do outside the pulpit. He urged the voters to support Gregory Hatcher, sportsman and regular fellow.

Sam Johnson told his son, "Get up there, Lyndon, and say something for Pat Neff."

So Lyndon Johnson mounted the truck that was being used as a speaker's stand. He started in his best college debater's style.

"You have heard a man say that Pat Neff doesn't hunt or fish," he began. "I want to remind you of the way these Austin sports come out into your hills and shoot your cattle when they're supposed to be hunting deer. I ask you if you want a city-slicking hunter who doesn't know a cow from a deer to be in charge of your railroad business and your bus line business and your oil business, or do you want a man

27

whose character is unimpeachable, and whose experience is already tested and proved?" And so forth.

Lyndon Johnson's first political speech went over big. His parents were proud of him, and said so. And when the votes were counted in that August primary, Pat Neff had defeated his opponent by more than 100,000 votes statewide, and had carried both Hays and Blanco counties, the two areas where the Johnsons worked for his cause.

A month later, Lyndon Johnson was teaching speech and history and coaching a debating team at Sam Houston High School in Houston, an unusually good job for a freshly minted graduate, especially in those early depression days.

As debate coach, Johnson found talent for his team. He groomed two students to perfection on both sides of the official debate question for 1930–31: "Resolved, that a substitute for the trial by jury should be adopted." Under the goading and prodding of their coach, the Sam Houston High School team won the county, district and state championships in the spring of 1931.

At that time, Blanco County was in the congressional district with a large chunk of South Texas, including the fabled King Ranch. When a special election came along in 1931 to fill the vacancy in that district, Lyndon Johnson made speeches in and around Blanco County in support of one of the King Ranch family, Richard Kleberg. When Kleberg won in the fall of 1931, he cast about for a "secretary," as administrative assistants were called in those days. Kleberg came to Austin to ask the advice of J. Alvin Wirtz, a lawyer who was prominent in politics. Wirtz told him that the young Johnson, who had worked for Kleberg, seemed ideally fit for the job. Kleberg made the offer and Lyndon Johnson accepted.

CHAPTER IV

Lyndon B. Johnson came to the nation's capital in the depths of the Great Depression. Both he and his boss, Congressman Richard Kleberg, were newcomers to Capitol Hill. They moved into a room in the old House Office Building, whose windows faced the inner court. The dark, Victorian furniture and high ceilings were redolent of history on the Potomac.

Representative Kleberg, wealthy and conservative rancher, kept his eager young secretary busy, but Lyndon Johnson found time to search out the facts and feel of Washington. He had a thousand questions on how things worked in Washington, who made them work, and why. As he became acquainted with other congressional aides, he besieged them with questions. The more he learned, the more he realized that Washington was where he belonged.

All day and far into the night Lyndon Johnson labored at the job of congressional secretary. In the process, and in off-duty time, he became a dominant figure among his fellow secretaries. Most of them were young and all of them were alert to the winds of change blowing through Washington; they argued and discussed and gossiped among themselves. None was more voluble and at the same time none was a better listener than the tall, thin, big-eared secretary to the Congressman from the 14th District.

Lyndon Johnson knew about the informal Little Congress, as the organization of congressional secretaries was called. One day, during a discussion of how it worked, another secretary in half-jest suggested that Lyndon Johnson try for election as Speaker of the Little Congress. The other secretary laughed to himself at the prospect of what the seniority system in that organization would do to this brash upstart from the Texas hills. The outcome, however, was the first example given Washington of the Johnson virtuosity in politics.

Johnson discovered that a large number of the congressional secretaries didn't take active part in its work and meetings, and thus were not committed to the incumbent hierarchy. He began to urge the inactive members to attend the meeting at which the election of Speaker was scheduled, and to vote for Lyndon Johnson. The tactic worked. His election as Speaker of the Little Congress is one of the few surprises ever to occur in that informal group.

One of his father's old friends from Austin was John Nance Garner, dominant Democrat in the House of Representatives before he became Vice President. Lyndon Johnson remembers Garner's advice to him after the victory in the Little Congress. "He told me," says Mr. Johnson, "that I needed to have friends on both sides of the aisle and that I wouldn't be worth much as Speaker if I didn't."

This exercise in practical politics by no means constituted the full range of Lyndon Johnson's political education during his four years as a Congressman's secretary.

To those who have seen it at close range, the procedure for getting things done in a government the size of ours appears to be mysterious, and, to the suspicious, perhaps unethical. Actually, it is simple for a man who assimilates information, makes friends, keeps his word, and pushes for what he wants. Johnson as a congressional secretary had superb basic training in this art of day-by-day government.

He learned that a friend is worth a thousand letters; that knowledge indeed is power; that a reputation for helping in return for help is the open sesame to nearly all the doors of bureaucracy; and that insistence, if properly applied, can speed up the normal pace of government business.

Congressman Sam Rayburn especially found in this eager, ambitious young man a ready listener and an intelligent interrogator. He imparted much of his wisdom to Lyndon Johnson. The way to make a good Congressman, Rayburn liked to say, is to pick a good man and keep him in office. The rules of seniority that prevent the U.S. Congress from flying into disorganized confusion put a premium on the man who continues to be re-elected. This tenure brings dividends to the districts that return their representatives in unbroken succession—dividends in terms of influence and membership on key committees. Mr. Rayburn's instinct was that of the professional, one who prefers to do his work with a minimum of confusion and effort, with a maximum of understanding and purpose and efficiency. It is an instinct that is lost on too many amateurs and on too many newcomers. It was not lost on young Lyndon Johnson.

Representative Kleberg was easily re-elected in 1932, the year Franklin D. Roosevelt and the Democrats swamped the Herbert Hoover Administration at the polls. This was a thrilling turn of events in Washington and Lyndon Johnson had a ringside seat. He saw new concepts of government arise, new ways of doing things emerge virtually overnight. He was close to the pulse of the nation when it changed from a flutter to a strong and steady beat.

Men have been arguing ever since about this bloodless revolution, about whether it should have happened at all, or whether it happened in the proper way. Many of those who weren't aware of it until it affected their personal affairs have never recovered from the shock. To such basically conservative men as Sam Rayburn and Lyndon Johnson, the New Deal was a sensible alternative to anarchy. It was the ultimate lesson up to that time in "can do." Think of it, in that period of ferment, and it was done.

The banking system and the home mortgages and home ownership and the system of private merchandising and all the other sinews of a free, capitalist nation were preserved intact by unorthodox emergency methods. It dramatized the fact that a nation can remain in the hands of its people in spite of the worst economic crisis in history, and if occasional dizzy mistakes went along with the rescue, these could be corrected whenever the people so decided. The green youngster from Texas matured as he saw that imagination could work in a seniority system, and that energetic leadership could make the difference. He never forgot what he learned.

Lyndon Johnson studied law for a year at Georgetown University in Washington during his congressional secretary tenure, but mostly he studied politics.

On occasional visits to Texas, and through visits by Texans to Washington, Lyndon Johnson continued to enlarge his circle of friends and acquaintances back home. In September, 1934, while in Austin, he dropped in early one morning at the office of Mrs. Gene Lassater to chat. Talking to Mrs. Lassater was a dark-haired, brown-eyed young lady, who was introduced to him as Claudia Taylor.

Claudia Taylor smiled and said Mrs. Lassater had already told her something about Lyndon Johnson. She had gone to Washington on a sight-seeing trip a few months before, and Mrs. Lassater had written the name Lyndon Johnson on a slip of paper, suggesting him as "a wonderful guy to show you the town." Claudia Taylor added that she was too shy to call a stranger and she just never did try to find him.

Then Lyndon Johnson asked Claudia Taylor to have breakfast with him. She accepted. Over breakfast he discovered that she, too, had graduated from high school at the age of fifteen, had lived in East Texas until she came to the University of Texas at Austin; that she had earned a bachelor of arts degree in 1933 and a bachelor of journalism only a few months before that morning, in 1934. He told her about his degree and his job with Representative Kleberg. The story is that after breakfast Lyndon Johnson drove Miss

31

Taylor by car to San Marcos to meet his parents, and not long afterward went to East Texas to be looked over by Thomas Jefferson Taylor, Claudia's father.

On November 17, 1934, two months after their first meeting, Lyndon Johnson and Claudia Taylor were married in San Antonio. They honeymooned in Mexico City. He was twenty-six, she was twenty-one.

Then it was time to return to Washington for the session of Congress starting in January, 1935. The proud bridegroom enjoyed introducing Mrs. Johnson to his friends in the capital as a person whose initials matched his own. For Claudia Alta Taylor had a nickname from infancy, bestowed by her nurse, who said "She's as pretty as a lady bird." And Lady Bird she was to all her friends.

"I knew I was married to something special, but I didn't know quite what," Mrs. Johnson says, recalling the whirl-wind courtship and sudden transplant to Washington. She set about managing the apartment household with quiet efficiency. Her husband's salary as secretary to Congressman Kleberg was $267 a month. Out of that she managed to buy an $18.75 savings bond every month. Her thrift and good management have continued for thirty years, even as her inheritances and business acumen have made her a multimillionairess.

The next turning point for Lyndon Johnson came six months after his marriage. Congress enacted a program to assist needy young people to learn trades and crafts, and to earn their way through college. It was called the National Youth Administration (NYA), to be set up on a state-by-state basis. The procedure called for establishing the kinds of work that would be offered to young men and women, finding supervisors and teachers for them, and agreeing with college administrations about requirements and jobs for students who would have to earn their way. No college in those depression days could afford to hire out of its own resources all the needy but deserving youngsters who wanted help. The first target was to get the National Youth Administration going in time to put students in school by September of 1935. It called for hard-driving, determined leadership.

Congressman Sam Rayburn is generally credited with bringing about the appointment of Lyndon B. Johnson as state NYA director for Texas. The challenge appealed to Johnson, former teacher and zealous in his desire to assist young people. He remembered vividly his own struggles to earn his college expenses. He knew how much a few extra

32

dollars at the right time could mean—actually the difference between staying in school or dropping out.

Lyndon Johnson returned to Texas in a hurry to start the NYA on its way. His assistant director was Willard Deason. Johnson lost no time recruiting other help. Sherman Birdwell of Austin recalls being summoned by Johnson to meet him in San Marcos at 7 A.M. in the Post Office Café. "His work day always started early," Birdwell said. Another who received the same invitation that morning was Jesse Kellam.

Birdwell was interested in a foreign service center and Kellam had a job with the Texas Education Agency when they sat down to breakfast with Lyndon Johnson. By the time the meal ended, they were both signed up for NYA.

They joined in establishing headquarters on the sixth floor of the Littlefield Building in Austin. "It was August and we were getting young people on the payroll so they could go to school in September," Birdwell recalls.

"'Put them to work, get them in school,' Lyndon kept hammering at us.

"The Littlefield building had is own electric power plant in those days, and its old gas lights were still usable. When the electricity went off at ten P.M., we'd fire up the gas lights and work on until two and three o'clock in the morning, then walk down six flights of stairs. Lyndon always was the last person to leave the office, whatever time it was."

At twenty-seven, Lyndon Johnson was the youngest state NYA director in the United States. By the time he had been at the job a year, his administration was being cited as a model to other state directors. Mrs. Franklin Roosevelt came to Austin to find out for herself how this young dynamo was providing work for so many youngsters. She saw the headquarters, inspected a girls' sewing room on East Sixth Street, and visited college campuses to observe students earning their expenses by working for their schools and being paid by NYA.

In the summer of 1936 when President Roosevelt visited the Texas Centennial Exposition, he drove from Fort Worth to Dallas. Along that highway a battalion of NYA workers was drawn up to salute FDR with their shovels, and at the front of the formation stood State Director Lyndon B. Johnson, saluting and smiling. In less than a year they were to meet again Texas, and in such a manner as to form a warm friendship.

The Lyndon Johnsons were lively participants in the conversational social life of young Austin people during the winter of 1936–37. They rented a house on San Gabriel

33

Street, in a wooded setting with a creek behind it, "a lovely place to sit in the dark" and talk about the great changes taking place in America. Their landlord was Dr. Robert Montgomery, brilliant, voluble, New-Dealing professor of economics at the University of Texas. The conversations and political arguments helped to crystallize the Johnson philosophy.

Even in those days, Lyndon Johnson's impulsive generosity was evident, as for example on an evening when Editor Charles Green of the Austin *American* visited the Johnsons. Green recalls that Johnson was wearing a pair of Mexican huaraches, open leather sandals. Green commented that the sandals seemed to be comfortable and certainly were handsome. Immediately Johnson pulled off the huaraches and insisted on Green's accepting them as a gift.

For the rest of 1936, Lyndon Johnson traveled throughout Texas, speaking to college groups and high school students, and to municipal and county authorities, promoting more ways to put more young people to work, earning and learning. NYA labor built many a public structure in those days, and laid out scores of roadside parks along Texas highways. As the program expanded, NYA built training centers with shops and dormitories so that vocational classes could be offered when local school systems could not provide them. The records show that about 33,000 Texas youths enrolled in NYA programs during the few years of the agency's work.

"If the Roosevelt Administration hadn't done anything else," Lyndon Johnson says, "its contribution to the young people of the nation through NYA would have justified it as a great administration."

As for the voters of Texas in 1936, the Roosevelt Administration was invincible. They whooped FDR to victory with a seven-to-one Texas majority as their contribution to his landslide over Republican Alfred Landon. This mandate helped set the stage for the next milestone in the life of Lyndon B. Johnson, the turning point that ultimately led him to the White House.

CHAPTER V

Geography, family history and personal background gave Lyndon Baines Johnson major advantages in his first political race. A knowledge of the Central Texas constituency to which he took his appeal for votes explains his head start.

The Tenth Congressional District of Texas sprawls horizontally across the center of the state's map: Austin, the capital, is the major city and population center of the ten counties. The other principal towns have always been farm-oriented.

The Johnson and Baines families have had roots in four counties: Blanco County where Johnson's grandfather started the ranch which evolved into the county seat, Johnson City; Washington County where the Rev. George Washington Baines preached and presided over a struggling school; Hays County, where his parents lived for more than one interval and where Lyndon Johnson attended college; and Travis County, where his grandfather and father both served in the Texas legislature and where Lyndon Johnson served as state administrator of the NYA when the opportunity to run for Congress arose.

Lyndon Johnson's farm and ranch upbringing couldn't have been more fitting for a young man who wanted to represent a district that was 70 per cent rural. The racial mixture of the district, including Germans, Bohemians, Poles, Wends, Swedes, Negroes and Latins, and dominated by the Anglo culture brought from the Old South, posed no barrier to a Johnson political campaign. Even then, he had an innate talent for projecting himself to all kinds of people. In addition, most of these people were bound together by a farm interest, and this was an interest that Johnson was adept at reaching.

Under Roosevelt's New Deal the national administration began touching nearly all the people of the Tenth District, whether they were farmers or small town merchants or college students or youngsters looking for work. The most spectacular effect of the New Deal on the Tenth District was the constructon of a series of dams designed to tame the Colorado River as it flowed down through the rugged hills past the state capital and across the coastal plain to the Gulf of Mexico. These dams would not only remove the threat of flood, but would also open new economic opportunities to virtually every resident of the Tenth District and many beyond it. Also, by making electric power cheaper, they promised to introduce conveniences which had been rare or unknown in this ranch country.

Tenth District Congressman James P. Buchanan, with his colleague from the neighboring Ninth District, Rep. J. J. Mansfield, had been the strongest supporter of this $20 million project. When he died of a heart attack on February 22, 1937, after twenty-four years in Congress, the Colorado dams program was in its first construction stage. One of the chief considerations, naturally, in the election of a successor, was to pick a man who knew enough about Washington and the New Deal to insure the completion of this work.

The implications of Congressman Buchanan's death were evident to J. Alvin Wirtz, the Austin lawyer most closely connected with the Colorado projects, and to Lyndon Johnson. Wirtz insisted that Johnson prepare at once to run in the special election.

On March 1, 1937, Lyndon Johnson announced his resignation as State NYA Director to become a candidate. He borrowed $10,000 from his father-in-law to meet campaign expenses. He had the promise of help from Alvin Wirtz in preparing speeches and in contacting influential Democrats in the ten counties. His issue was ready-made: 100 per cent support of President Roosevelt.

The controversy all over the United States about Mr. Roosevelt's proposal to enlarge the United States Supreme Court—to "pack the court," his opponents called it—was at its height in March, 1937. So Johnson had more than identification with a successful New Deal agency going for him: he could get full attention any time he mentioned the President's Supreme Court plan. Lyndon Johnson said he was behind the President, court plan and every other plan.

He chose San Marcos as the scene for his opening campaign speech. His family and friends came in droves to hear him unfurl the Roosevelt program boldly. He advertised his own contacts and experience in Washington as ideal background for a "can do" Congressman. Johnson boasted that he was the first candidate to embrace the FDR court plan, the first one courageous enough to take sides quickly.

Five other candidates filed for places on the special election ballot. Two of them, Merton Harris and Polk Shelton, ran as pro-Roosevelt candidates but without the Johnson energy and zest. C. N. Avery, who had been Buchanan's political manager for many years, made the race, and State Senator Houghton Brownlee came in. Senator Brownlee started with the handicap of having signed a resolution a few weeks earlier in the Texas Senate opposing the Roosevelt court proposal. Avery also took the conservative tack.

Lyndon Johnson found friendly support all over the district. Besides his family ties, he knew many young people whom he had helped to get jobs. They and their families needed little urging to support him.

In a little more than four weeks of campaigning, Lyndon Johnson criss-crossed the ten-county Tenth District on a dawn-to-midnight schedule. He spoke at more than two hundred political meetings; went into stores and up and down the streets of the towns, introducing himself, asking for votes. On most of his forays Mrs. Johnson accompanied him, but she had not overcome her shyness, as she later did, to become a political campaigner.

In addition to his face-to-face campaigning in the villages and towns of the district, Lyndon Johnson spoke over the radio to advertise the Tenth's need for a 100 per cent New Deal Congressman.

The secretaries in Alvin Wirtz's office and the volunteer workers in the Johnson campaign headquarters, almost bewildered in the hurry-hurry atmosphere generated by the candidate, gave him a nickname: the Blanco Blitz.

The Austin newspaper, not taking sides in this special election, ran a page one poll inviting readers to cast straw votes for or against Mr. Roosevelt's court proposal. The result was a lopsided total in favor of FDR which added force to the Johnson campaign.

Two days before the election Lyndon Johnson suffered an attack of appendicitis and underwent emergency surgery. A friend broadcast for him the speech that had been prepared for the closing campaign rally, while the patient listened from his hospital bed.

On April 10, the voters of the Tenth District chose Lyndon Johnson and his New Deal platform by a convincing plurality: he had more than twice the votes of any of the other candidates.

Because of the strong feeling about the FDR court battle, Johnson's election made front-page news all over the country. FDR had already announced plans for a cruise in the Gulf of Mexico and a return to Washington by train, starting from Texas. After reading the headlines, he told Governor James V. Allred of Texas to be sure the young New Deal congressional victor would be presented to him.

Lyndon Johnson recovered from his operation in time to accompany Governor Allred aboard the presidential yacht at

Galveston. Johnson wore an orchid in his lapel for the event. Mr. Roosevelt took the new Congressman to ride across Texas with him on the presidential train.

On that journey, the President and the eager young Texan began a friendship that endured for the remaining eight years of FDR's life and left a deep influence on the character of Lyndon B. Johnson. When Johnson was about to leave the train at the state border, Mr. Roosevelt gave him a Washington telephone number and asked him to use it when he came to be sworn into the House of Representatives. The number turned out to be that of Thomas Corcoran, "Tommy the Cork," of the FDR inner circle. Roosevelt's gratitude took another, more tangible form. After taking the oath of office on May 14, 1937, Johnson heard the clerk drone out a list of appointments. Suddenly his own name was called out as a member of the House Naval Affairs Committee. It was a plum for a freshman in the House, given him at Roosevelt's request.

Sam Johnson, naturally, was filled with pride over his son's election to Congress. Mr. Johnson had been out of the Texas legislature for a dozen years, and had been employed during most of that time as an inspector for the Texas Railroad Commission. He had, however, only a short period to enjoy his son's success. He died in October, 1937, while his son was home from his first session of Congress.

It was the first break in the close-knit Johnson family. From that time forward, Lyndon Johnson drew ever closer to his mother. During her remaining twenty years of life, Rebekah Johnson often found herself, at her son's request, giving her judgment on ideas for speeches, political tactics, or family matters.

One day, setting out to speak to a gathering of Texans of Bohemian descent in another county, he called on his mother. "Mama, tell me what I ought to say," he pleaded. Mrs. Johnson wrote on a sheet of paper a summary of the history of Bohemian settlements in Texas and the names of some of their outstanding leaders. When she finished, Lyndon Johnson had all he needed for a speech that would appeal directly to his individual audience.

Congressman Johnson brought his brother, Sam Houston Johnson, who is five years younger, to help out in greeting constituents at his office at Washington, and later gave his sister Rebekah a clerical position in the nation's capital.

The real training of Lyndon Johnson in how to be a Congressman came from such canny, patient mentors as Vice President John Garner, Democratic Whip Sam Rayburn, and their veteran colleagues. They took their new Texas associate into the quiet, late-afternoon meetings where strategy was planned, where the various ways of persuading fellow Congressmen were discussed, and where occasionally Mr. Garner would lead in "striking a blow for liberty"—his term for having a drink of whiskey.

In those conversations, Lyndon Johnson saw patience demonstrated and canny planning in practice. The Texas members of Congress worked together as a team on nearly all matters affecting their state. Divergent in viewpoints, they respected each other and helped each other on a practical basis. Lyndon Johnson had seen this from the office of Congressman Kleberg during secretarial years. Now he was a part of it, and it fit him like a glove.

Johnson needed few lessons in how to strengthen and broaden his contacts with the voters in the Tenth District. From his first day in Washington, he laid down the rule that all letters would be answered the day they were received, if at all possible, and would be answered promptly no matter what their request or content. He had no difficulty maintaining the flow of federal funds into the district. In particular, he made sure that the Colorado River program of dams and generators continued to receive full funding. Soil conservation programs and farm credit programs, including the first legislation designed to help Negro farmers, had Congressman Johnson's support. Johnson even voted against President Roosevelt and Representative Rayburn on one test involving continuation of low-cost loans to farmers. Johnson voted for the farmers.

Congressman Buchanan had arranged for the $4,500,000 financing of the first big dam on the Colorado, the one that today bears his name. Congressman Johnson followed through by securing Bureau of Reclamation financing to a total of $15,500,000 for the lakes downstream.

During the conferences necessitated by the complexity of the river program, Lyndon Johnson's quick mind and ability to grasp instantly the central part of any problem aroused anew the admiration of Lawyer Wirtz, who was general counsel for the river authority board.

"I've seen engineers and rate experts start explaining a detailed matter to Lyndon," Mr. Wirtz liked to recall, "and he'd show complete understanding before they got halfway through talking, and he'd be asking for the next problem. He had the quickest, most analytical mind I've even seen."

The story is told, too, about an episode in the power negotiations, in which Mr. Wirtz sat down with private utility executives to work out one of the touchy problems. Congressman Johnson was by his side in the meeting. The discussion became quite heated. The young Congressman told a utility executive to "go to hell." It broke up the meeting. Mr. Wirtz sadly reminded Johnson:

1. That while a man could tell another to go to hell, he couldn't make him go, and

2. That the net effect of the outburst was to shatter a negotiation which Wirtz had spent much pains and strategy to bring about.

Crestfallen and contrite, Johnson apologized, and helped bring the matter some time later to a successful conclusion. It was a lasting lesson in judgment.

Lyndon Johnson was re-elected to Congress in 1938, and again in 1940 without opposition. This was plain proof that his ceaseless efforts to keep in touch with the people of the Tenth District—by letter, by personal visits, by pushing for legislation they wanted passed—produced results. In addition to his widely advertised support of the Colorado River projects, he led the way under the Rural Electrification Administration (REA) act of 1935 in helping farmers and ranchers to form cooperatives and bring electric power to their homes and barns.

The young Congressman was no theorist on electric energy for rural residents. He remembered his years of toil on the business end of a well pump, on the hand-powered clippers that sheared goats and sheep, on milking cows by hand. He also remembered best the grimy chore of cleaning and filling kerosene lamps, and the dim light they gave for reading and writing.

Those who opposed the government REA program tried to insist that the people out in the country wouldn't pay money for electric energy, that they would rather keep on with their age-old hand methods of labor and save the dollars. Lyndon Johnson knew this wasn't true. He had a standing offer to buy any man a Stetson hat who found a farmer or rancher refusing to pay the price of bringing electricity to his place. Nobody ever claimed the hat.

In 1938, Johnson received a letter from an old friend at Floresville, Editor Sam Fore, an important constituent of Johnson's old boss, Congressman Kleberg. Fore wrote of an exceptional Floresville youngster named John Connally, and asked Johnson to help Connally get a job so he could complete his studies at the University of Texas. Congressman Johnson saw to it that John Connally obtained a job from the National Youth Administration at Austin. Connally not only earned his degree at the University of Texas but proved his political talent by winning election as president of the student body in his senior year. This talent led him to the governorship of Texas in 1962. Johnson offered the young graduate a position in his congressional staff and John Connally accepted. He joined the Johnson staff as chief administrative assistant in Washington in 1939.

"John Connally taught me how to shake hands," Johnson said afterward. The Johnson handshake up to then had been a hasty finger grasp. From the time of the Connally lesson, it became full and firm, with an extra squeeze on occasion.

Lyndon Johnson's unopposed status in the election year of 1940 gave him time to take an active part in the tense maneuvering that resulted in selection of Texas' delegation to the Democratic National Convention that year. Texas Democratic leaders divided on the question of a third term for Franklin D. Roosevelt. The Texas congressional delegation split on the same rock. The question to be settled in Texas was whether the state's delegation would go to Chicago instructed to "stop Roosevelt." The pro-FDR elements argued vigorously that the war in Europe, now blazing to its first climax, meant just one thing: Mr. Roosevelt must be renominated and re-elected. The opposition revered the two-term tradition, and could not support a presidential third term for any reason. As an articulate third-termer, Lyndon Johnson helped fashion the compromise on which the state convention finally agreed: Send the delegation to Chicago pledged to support John Nance Garner for President but instructed not to take part in any "stop-Roosevelt" bloc that might form.

After FDR had been nominated for his third term, the national party leadership had another assignment for Lyndon Johnson. There were important congressional contests all over the country that fall. The experts forecast that the Republican Party would come to life after eight years and win extra strength in the House. At the request of his friends in the House, and with Mr. Roosevelt's blessing, Johnson took on the chore of channeling party funds and party workers to the crucial congressional districts in an effort to head off Republican gains.

Congressman Johnson's vantage point as a White House favorite, and his widening acquaintance in Democratic Party leadership ranks, gave him opportunities to work beyond the immediate concerns of his own district. The events of 1940 set him on the road to prominence in the national Democratic Party, a road he traveled energetically for the next twenty-three years.

Johnson's work consisted principally of hanging onto a battery of telephones, checking the situations in the embattled districts, sending money and ideas and phoning key Democrats advice about strategy and tactics wherever they were needed. So well did he disburse about $100,000 in campaign funds, and an untold amount of advice and exhortation, that when the votes came in, the Democrats had gained seats and the Republicans had lost a net of six congressional places.

When FDR swept to his third term in the presidency, bolstered by this gain in Congress, he turned full-time to preparations for the war he considered inevitable. In all the White House strategy sessions seeking answers to the vociferous isolationist spokesmen who were bemusing the country, Lyndon Johnson sat in with keen and informed interest.

In April, 1941, the death of Senator Morris Sheppard of Texas left an opening which FDR and Johnson quickly attempted to exploit.

CHAPTER VI

In the spring of 1941, the Nazi juggernaut crunched through the Balkans, Greece, and Crete. On the domestic scene labor strife erupted in the coal mines, the aircraft factories, and shipyards. In the fumbling federal efforts to mobilize for war, there were quarrels between the Administration and the men who capitalized and operated the basic industries. The draft act was only a few months old, its future in doubt.

Texas political leadership growled in warring camps, muttering over the bitterness left from the 1940 third-term struggle. Although the state's voters had gone solidly for Franklin D. Roosevelt, there wasn't a real friend of FDR in high state office in Texas. Many Rooseveltians still held rank in the Democratic Party of Texas, but the official machinery of state government was manned by those who were either hostile or indifferent to the man in the White House. They had won office in 1938 and in 1940 by campaigns which ignored national and international affairs.

The President and the men around him began to increase their efforts to communicate the prospects of a future conflict. But the isolationist chorus in the United States Senate had the spotlight for preaching peace at any price. They vigorously took anti-preparedness positions on every question of foreign policy.

Senator Morris Sheppard's death presented an opportunity to the White House to drive a wedge of its own into the state. True enough, the state's National Guard troops had been called to active duty. Some new military and naval installations had been created in various parts of the state, and thousands of young Texans already had volunteered for armed service. But the state's civilian tempo had changed little. Its political leaders did not appear interested in becoming informed about the nation's predicament.

Soon after Senator Sheppard's funeral, the young ex-football hero, Attorney General Gerald Mann, announced his candidacy in the special election that would fill the unexpired Senate term. On his heels came Congressman Martin Dies, known for his leadership of the House un-American Investigating Committee.

The Governor, W. Lee O'Daniel, sprang a characteristic shocker by appointing the aged, infirm Andrew Jackson Houston, eighty-six, to take the Senate seat from that date until after the election. This appointment of the last surviving son of Texas' number one hero, Sam Houston, was regarded as a sure sign that the Governor intended to run for the Senate as soon as he could extricate himself from a running battle with the legislature.

Lyndon Johnson thereupon paid a well-publicized visit to President Roosevelt in the White House. He stood in FDR's presence to tell reporters that he would enter the Senate race. A smiling FDR received the reporters' questions in a bantering manner and then authorized this direct quotation:

"There are three things to be said about the senate contest in Texas. First, it is up to the people of Texas to elect the man they want as their Senator; second, everybody knows that I cannot enter a state election; and third, to be truthful, all I can say is, Lyndon is a very old, old friend of mine."

The launching of his candidacy from the White House put Johnson on page one in all the newspapers of Texas. He was almost unknown outside his own district, but he mobilized help in a hurry. Texans working in Washington resigned to come home and take part in the campaign. Harold Young, a Department of Agriculture official, and J. Alvin Wirtz, then Undersecretary of the Interior, headed the list.

As the official Roosevelt candidate, Johnson found himself in the Texas political big leagues. He was surrounded by a caliber of support he had never enjoyed before. Publishers, businessmen and lawyers intent on helping Roosevelt in his preparedness policies, and New Deal Democrats from sections of the state far from his own district, joined the Johnson campaign. Among these men Johnson made many important friends who have had much to do with his political successes ever since 1941.

Raymond Buck, Fort Worth businessman, became the official campaign chairman. Publishers Charles E. Marsh of Austin and E. S. Fentress of Waco, with interests in a number of Texas newspapers, put major resources behind Lyndon Johnson. So did Houston Harte, another wide-ranging Texas newspaper publisher.

Marsh, who had come to admire his own Congressman since his first election and who was a confidant of the then Vice President Henry Wallace, traveled with Johnson on most of his strenuous journeys back and forth across the state. Marsh's talent with words and his skill at appealing to public emotions contributed in a major way to Johnson's central campaign theme stressing the need by President Roosevelt

44

for a young, energetic, well-informed Senator to help build up America's strength.

Once again Johnson chose his old college town, San Marcos, as the scene of his opening campaign speech. A throng of 6,000 gathered that evening to hear the fiery young Congressman shout "Roosevelt and Unity" as his battle cry. He enlarged vociferously on the theme that the national peril called for sacrifices from all elements of the nation, an end to political back-biting and feuding, and a closing of ranks behind Franklin D. Roosevelt.

"Franklin D. and Lyndon B.," someone yelled, and the campaigners had their slogan to plaster all over the shop windows and windshields of Texas.

Johnson's advisers mapped a man-killing itinerary. They wore out relays of drivers as the Johnson caravan rolled from town to town on a day-and-night schedule of open-air speeches and radio broadcasts.

Johnson detested the formal speeches which radio required for clearance in advance. If he were making the broadcast before a crowd, he delighted in finishing the script, throwing it over his shoulder, peeling off his coat, and saying, "Now, let's get down to my country-boy style of talking."

Johnson's campaign used liberally the entertainment touches that had become stylized in Texas politics with the 1938 advent of W. Lee O'Daniel. Singers, string bands, and trumpet players helped attract crowds.

Governor O'Daniel finally essayed a traveling campaign, but between bad luck with spring thunderstorms and the heckling from the legislature which kept him close to Austin, he had to depend largely on radio broadcasts. Those, however, were his forte; he had the state's best-known hillbilly band, which included his two sons and his daughter.

The campaigns of Gerald Mann and Martin Dies were colorless by comparison.

Johnson hammered the "Roosevelt and Unity" theme along with his own record for being able "to get things done" in Congress. He pictured himself as the only experienced, ready-to-serve candidate in the race. Before it was over, he had all the candidates saying defensively that they certainly were for Mr. Roosevelt as the national leader in time of peril, and indeed they believed in 100 per cent or, for that matter, 200 per cent preparedness to keep war off our shores. O'Daniel even wired FDR an offer to create a completely independent Texas army, navy, and air force as the state's contribution to a strong America. The story made news, but Mr. Roosevelt's quick rejoinder, "Preposterous," made more news.

45

The gambling odds at the start of the race rated Lyndon Johnson one chance in ten for election. By the end of the campaign, just before election, he stood at even money with the professional bettors. Statewide polls of voter sentiment put him neck and neck with Governor O'Daniel, the magician of the microphone, who had whipped everybody in sight in two recent gubernatorial elections.

But there were two factors that did not show up in the opinion polls and on which even the most frenzied campaigning had no effect. First, 1941 was an off-year, politically, in Texas. This is the term describing the odd-numbered years when no regular elections are scheduled and when, especially in that era, the pressure to qualify for voting was not felt. The number of eligible voters in the year 1941 was much less than in the preceding regular election year. The second factor revolved around the ambitions of the lieutenant governor, Coke R. Stevenson, to become governor. If W. Lee O'Daniel won the Senate race, Stevenson automatically become governor and had a year and a half to serve before facing a full-fledged election.

Stevenson, a tall, rancher-lawyer, tanned and taciturn, had a statewide following, painstakingly built up over the years. In addition, he and his leaders had a working relationship with the old fox of Texas politics, James E. Ferguson. "Farmer Jim" Ferguson had been governor, was impeached in 1917, then years later caused his wife, "Ma" Ferguson, to be elected twice as governor.

Johnson's energetic campaign got under the skin of the Stevenson-Ferguson forces to the point that Farmer Jim himself signed newspaper advertisements during the final week of the race in which he urged all Coke Stevenson's friends to vote for O'Daniel—not that the Governor really needed help, he said, but just to make it a "double-barreled cinch" that Coke Stevenson would become governor. It was the first sign of life from Jim Ferguson in a number of years, but he was still remembered and powerful.

Johnson kept up the pace that caused his staff to call him the "Blanco Blitz." Through West Texas on one campaign swing, flood waters from swollen streams ran up to the hub caps of the car. His airplane flights dared weather and cowpasture airports. He had a recurring throat trouble and a skin rash brought on by nervous tension. He was playing to win.

For forty-eight hours after the votes were cast, it looked as if he had done it. On the morning after Election Day, Johnson's lead was 5,000 votes over O'Daniel. In a telephone conversation with Alvin Wirtz, the young candidate said that it seemed fairly solid to him.

"Just wait," said Wirtz drily. "By tomorrow you won't have anywhere near five thousand votes lead."

His estimate proved more than accurate. In the early morning hours of the second day, more votes for O'Daniel began to turn up in "corrected" returns from rural counties scattered across the state. On the third day, Johnson's lead was cut to seventy-seven votes, and on the fourth day the final count of nearly 600,000 ballots showed O'Daniel to be the winner by 1,311 votes.

Johnson refused to call for any rechecking or investigation of the curious post-election reversal of the vote trend. He went back to his congressional duties.

By the time his campaign ended, President Roosevelt had declared an unlimited national emergency, had used troops to break the aviation workers' strike in California, and the Soviet Union had been invaded by the Nazis.

When the Japanese attacked Pearl Harbor on December 7, 1941, Johnson immediately entered the U.S. Navy as a reserve officer.

He was restive under the office duties first assigned him as a lieutenant commander, USNR. Within a few weeks he managed to secure an overseas mission. He was sent to the South Pacific as a member of a survey team to gather field information on the performance of military equipment and the effectiveness of military supply procedures.

Lieutenant Commander Johnson flew aerial missions on Navy and Army airplanes. On one flight in a Navy patrol bomber on which he was an official observer, Johnson saw Japanese fighter-plane bullets knocks out one of the bomber's engines and inflict gaping wounds on some of the crew members. The pilot barely managed to bring the crippled bomber back to its New Guinea base. General Douglas MacArthur decorated Johnson with a Silver Star Medal for his conduct on this mission.

Another plane on which one of Johnson's colleagues from Washington, an Army colonel, was an observer, was shot down with the loss of all aboard. Johnson later survived a crash landing aboard the famous Army Air Corps bomber, *The Swoose,* in an isolated part of Australia. William L. White's book, *Queens Die Proudly,* quotes a crew member of *The Swoose* relating what happened after the crash landing:

We got out. Pretty soon Australian ranchers began crawling out of holes in the ground—I don't know where else they came from—and right away Lieutenant Commander Johnson gets busy. He begins to get acquainted.

They tell him where we are, and some of them go off to get a truck to take us into town where we can telephone, and more keep coming, and Johnson is shaking hands all around, and he comes back and tells us these are real folks—the best damn folks in the world, except maybe the folks in his own Texas.

Pretty soon he knows all their first names, and they are telling him why there ought to be a high tariff on wool, and there is no question he swung that country for Johnson before he left. He was in his element. I know he sure swung *The Swoose* crew. He can carry that precinct any day. . . .

Johnson was still in uniform when the Texas elections of 1942 came on. Petitions signed by more than 22,000 voters in the Tenth Texas District asked that his name appear on the ballot for re-election to Congress. It was done, and nobody attempted to oppose his candidacy. He learned about this in Australia weeks after it happened.

President Roosevelt soon afterward ordered all members of Congress who were on active military service to return to their congressional duties. When Johnson got back to Washington, he told everybody who would listen that while American soldiers, sailors, and marines were second to none in quality, the state of their equipment and ordnance left much to be desired. He made more than one public statement excoriating "stuffed shirt generals and admirals" and called for leadership unafraid to cut red tape.

"We must get rid of the indecisive, stupid, selfish, and incompetent in high military positions. . . . We are going to give our men leadership and equipment superior to that of any in the world. We are going to have to move quickly to coordinate dive bombers and domestic politics, tanks and military strategy, ships and the will of the people. Management and manpower are going to have to be closely woven into a smoothly functioning machine devoid of squabbles and petty jealousies. . . ."

His fervor for tightening up the war effort found an outlet in his chairmanship of a special subcommittee of the House Naval Affairs Committee with the mission of searching out wasteful practices in procurement, manpower and policies.

During Lyndon Johnson's active duty in the Navy, Mrs. Johnson had refreshed her college training in stenographic skills and had taken over the management of the Congressman's office. She served without pay for the seven months he was away. It gave her new insights into the political skill required, and which her husband had shown, in his efforts to be the busiest Congressman in town.

It also set Mrs. Johnson to thinking that she wouldn't mind becoming a business woman herself if the opportunity arose, as it soon did.

In 1943 came the first of two inheritances to Mrs. Johnson. It was a modest sum but large enough to pose for Lyndon and Lady Bird Johnson the question of using it wisely.

"We had never really faced up to what would happen to us if I were defeated in politics," Johnson recalls. "My wife had a degree in journalism from the University of Texas. She always thought she could get a job on a newspaper if she had to. I had taught school a little while but I wasn't competent to go back to that; and when I thought about it all, I figured I could make a living as a salesman."

The inheritance gave them a chance to invest for the future. Their first impulse was to purchase a newspaper. "I figured my wife could be the editor and I could sell the advertising." They priced a newspaper which was for sale, but finally decided against buying it because it was too far away from his district.

Then the Johnsons heard about a radio station in their own home town of Austin. This station, KTBC, was on the rocks and could be had at a bargain. Here Johnson thought first of his respect for his friends who owned the daily newspapers in Austin, Charles E. Marsh and E. S. Fentress.

Johnson wrote and asked them whether they thought the station was worth the price, and whether they would object to the Johnsons entering a business that would be competitive with their own newspaper advertising sales staff. Both answered that the proposed investment seemed worth a try, and that they welcomed the prospective new radio ownership to the business life of Austin.

Then Johnson tracked down an old friend and associate from NYA days, Jesse Kellam. The Johnsons persuaded Kellam to come into the radio enterprise as manager, with Mrs. Johnson as head of the firm.

"Lady Bird took one look at the layout and said, 'I don't know much about radio but I do know something about cleaning house,' " Kellam remembers. "She bought a pair of coveralls, a bunch of brooms and mops and some soap, and for a solid week she worked on that little walkup, two-room radio station until it fairly sparkled. It was my job to go around town and pay all the bills that had piled up in the name of KTBC. The bankers were glad to see me coming.

"She worked eighteen hours a day for five months before we brought the station into the black," Kellam says.

The following year the Johnsons became parents for the first time. Their daughter, Lynda Bird, was born in Washington in 1944. It was the same year that Johnson was returned again without opposition to his seat in Congress. The radio station grew and prospered. They acquired a bit of real estate in Austin. Their fortunes were on the rise.

Then President Roosevelt died. One of Johnson's staff members wailed, "What will become of us? There's no one left." Johnson replied quietly, "There's Mr. Truman."

The war was over and domestic politics once more moved into the spotlight. Then came Lyndon Johnson's first re-election contest within the Tenth District. Conservative elements, tired of his brash New Deal posture and suspicious of his prosperity, decided it was time to elect a less rambunctious Congressman. The choice to oppose Johnson was a man named Hardy Hollers.

The opposition was well-financed, but not particularly well organized. Its strategy boiled down to a series of bitter attacks on Johnson as a politician accused of feathering his own nest by virtue of his New Deal influence. Johnson relied heavily on his record of service and on the need for an experienced Congressman to help the district adjust to postwar strains.

Though no Congressman welcomes an opposing candidate, Johnson met his first competition for the Tenth District seat with a certain relish. It gave him the opportunity to marshal his troops and put them to work. Characteristically, Johnson himself worked and worried harder and longer than even his most devoted aides. By telephone, by radio, by newspaper appeal and in person, he carried on his campaign. He had files dating from 1937 listing the names of every person and every family assisted or contacted during his tenure. His letter-writing brigade pecked out streams of personalized communications to these voters.

Lyndon Johnson won his first contested race for Congress since 1937 by a convincing majority, but the attacks on him during that campaign cut him deeply. He had devoted his every energy for nine years to working for the people of the Tenth District. He simply could not understand how any of them came to oppose him.

For at that time, and for some years to come, politics and service to the constituents formed his sole interest. Johnson worked long hours, seven days a week, talked and thought nothing but the business of his congressional office. This made him a superb Congressman who could intercede for people who had problems with a federal agency, who could bring home the appropriations and the programs. He was a perfectionist in his field, and to be unappreciated by even one constituent for all that, shocked him deeply.

He thought long and hard about whether to continue in politics or whether to seek another outlet for his furious energy. It was hard for him to grasp the old American tradition that citizens tend to look with condescension, and too often with contempt, on the people they elect to serve them. To a man as sensitive as Lyndon Johnson, eager to help and please even total strangers, this old tradition as applied to him felt like a blow in the solar plexus.

CHAPTER VII

The mood of doubt about a political future continued to press on Lyndon Johnson during 1947 and 1948. The ding-dong battle between President Harry Truman and the Republican majority in Congress did nothing to lift Johnson's spirits. He voted against Mr. Truman on the passage of the Taft-Hartley Act, and voted to override the Truman veto of it. He made no bones about his distaste for the Truman version of a civil rights program, although he wasn't in the mainstream of that controversy.

The Johnsons found new joy in the birth of their second daughter, Lucy, in 1947. The presence of two baby girls in the household put a new dimension in the daily routine which for so long had revolved solely around the Congressman's work.

In Texas, conservative Democrats continued to rule. Many of the young men who had helped Lyndon Johnson win re-election to Congress began to talk, during the ensuing two years, about the necessity of doing something to break up what they considered stodgy, old guard state leadership. When U.S. Senator W. Lee O'Daniel let it be known that he would not seek re-election in 1948, the pot began to simmer.

Soon after O'Daniel's intended retirement from the Senate became known, Coke Stevenson, who had retired as governor after five years in office, and his friends decided that Stevenson was the ideal choice to replace O'Daniel as he had replaced him in 1941 in the state gubernatorial chair. This crystallized the young men's determination.

There were only a few of them involved in the active discussion of a possible candidate to oppose Coke Stevenson, and all were close associates of Congressman Johnson: John Connally, former assistant to Johnson, campaigner for him in the ill-fated 1941 senatorial race as well as in the successful 1946 congressional race, an up-and-coming young lawyer and businessman, a decorated U. S. Navy combat veteran; J. J. Pickle, another Navy veteran, and a one-time NYA executive under Johnson, now a public relations counsel and political wheelhorse; Stuart Long, newspaperman and U. S. Marine Corps veteran, active in Johnson's political organization in Austin.

There were a few others. All shared the feeling that it was imperative to enter a candidate against Stevenson.

When Johnson came to Austin in the spring of 1948 to look over his problems of re-election to Congress these friends went to work trying to persuade him to give up that seat and try again for the United States Senate.

Lyndon Johnson was not in much of a mood to listen. He had not forgotten his grueling Senate race against W. Lee O'Daniel. He was familiar with Stevenson's smashing successes in two gubernatorial elections and his general popularity over the state. The magic name of FDR was gone from the hustings and there was no other magic to replace it in 1948. Johnson knew that Stevenson had begun his leisurely campaign in January, had a built-in state-wide organization of people appointed to important local positions all over Texas during his eight years as governor. Johnson had made no state-wide effort or impact since 1941.

Johnson's friends came to him one night at his home in Austin, shortly before the deadline for filing candidacies in the Democratic primary of 1948. One of them remembers the scene vividly.

"We talked and talked, trying to prove to him that he could beat Stevenson. We taunted him. We sweet-talked him. We tried every argument any of us could think of. Lyndon just wouldn't agree to run for the Senate."

Finally, Johnson went to bed and left his friends arguing.

"We decided to run John Connally," says a participant in the discussion. "This was in 1948, remember. All the Connallys are tall and handsome. We were going to get six surplus command cars, and put John and his father and brothers in each of them and send them over the state, campaigning by public address systems on the cars."

This was the plan when they finally went to rest that night.

"Next morning," the narrator continues, "we told Lyndon that since he wouldn't run, we wanted him to help us elect John.

"That afternoon, Lyndon called a press conference in the penthouse of the Driskill Hotel to announce himself as a candidate for the United States Senate. We decided later that what influenced him was the thought that if we figured John Connally, who had never run for political office, could win, Johnson sure enough could win—but, of course, that is reading minds in retrospect. . . ."

Lyndon Johnson faced an uphill struggle from the start of his 1948 race for the Democratic nomination for United States Senator from Texas. By the time he made his opening campaign address, there were ten other candidates in the field. The best-known, of course, was Coke Stevenson. Another aspirant with more than ordinary support was George E. B. Peddy of Houston, a big-city conservative, lawyer and businessman. The other candidates merely cluttered up the scene.

Johnson's opening speech in his drive for the Senate nomination offered a program of Peace, Progress and Prosperity. No particular notice was paid to it, and it more or less evaporated in the general political confusion. Just then he suffered a kidney ailment and was flown to the Mayo Clinic in Minnesota for two weeks' treatment.

Lyndon Johnson emerged from the hospital with new ideas. Increasing Soviet hostility in Eastern Europe and the consequent threat of another war made preparedness a new issue in the Texas political scramble. Johnson seized on it quickly. He presented himself as the most experienced candidate in the field of military problems. He managed to imply that he was the only Senate aspirant who clearly had never been isolationist.

Candidate Johnson played other strings, too: the need for more than $31 a month to old age pensioners, the need for more water conservation and better soil management, the need for energetic Lyndon Johnson to go to the Senate.

He procured a helicopter, had its name, *The Johnson City Windmill,* painted on the sides, and set out to rouse the electorate from on high. His 1941 nucleus of Alvin Wirtz, Raymond Buck, and John Connally provided headquarters leadership. They found many old Roosevelt Democrats ready to take local roles in promoting Lyndon Johnson's candidacy.

His helicopter barnstorming caused much excitement across Texas. Johnson had loudspeaker horns mounted on the whirlybird. He delighted to hover over the center of a small town and broadcast his appeal downward to the neck-craning citizens. He often landed in a farmer's field where work was going on. He'd leap out of *The Johnson City Windmill,* approach the startled farmer at a dog trot, wring his hand, ask for his vote, run back to the helicopter and take off. Occasionally, if he saw a freight train waiting at a siding, he'd pop down from the sky and electioneer among the train crew men.

Riding with Johnson in the helicopter toward the end of the campaign was Horace Busby, a young University of Texas student who left his classes temporarily to join the candidate. It was the beginning of a long association, for Horace Busby became, and is today, one of Lyndon Johnson's closest advisers, as well as idea man and speech writer.

Often, Johnson visited more than twenty towns, villages, and farms in a day's helicopter journeying. If headwinds or refueling slowed him down, singers and comedians kept the crowd until he could windmill in to the scene.

While the candidate hopped and whirled around Texas, Mrs. Johnson, though she had not yet completely conquered her shyness, occasionally tried her hand at asking strangers to vote for her husband. When she drove across country, whether on personal errands or to meet with women's groups, she bought only five gallons of gasoline at a time so she'd have an excuse to stop at more filling stations and ask the attendants to vote for her husband. A friend remembers riding with Mrs. Johnson from Houston northward one day on a "five-gallon" tour. When they reached the second stop for gasoline, Mrs. Johnson turned to her companion and said, "Mary, you ask them this time. I just can't do it again."

In late June, about a month before the first primary election day, the state hierarchy of the American Federation of Labor endorsed Coke Stevenson in a public move that surprised Lyndon Johnson as much as it surprised most other Texans. Johnson's long affiliation with the New Deal and all its works, the casual observers thought, would have made him first choice for any labor union group. Johnson's support of the Taft-Hartley Law, however, had put him on labor's blacklist.

Johnson made much of the labor endorsement of Mr. Stevenson, asking from the stump several times a day whether his rival had made a secret agreement with the labor union group to try, if elected, to secure repeal of the Taft-Hartley Law. Johnson hammered this theme day and night for the rest of the campaign.

Whether because of this issue, or of his energetic vote-seeking, or both, Johnson found himself with the second highest total of ballots in the field of eleven candidates when the first primary election results came in. He and Coke Stevenson faced each other then in a runoff election with a scant month to work over the voters again.

By the time the runoff campaign began, the first Berlin blockade focused Texas attention more closely on European war clouds. The national draft was resumed. A stronger national defense posture, which Johnson had been preaching for six weeks, became even more popular. He abandoned his helicopter as being too slow for the final three-weeks' campaigning, and began to travel to the major cities of Texas by airplane. He continued also to use radio network time to keep his campaign coverage statewide no matter where he might be. The contrast between Lyndon Johnson, personification of action, and Coke R. Stevenson, deliberate and slow-going rancher, was vividly presented to the voters.

When returns from the second primary balloting on August 28 began to come in, the totals for each man mounted side by side. They were never more than a few votes apart. At 1 A.M. on August 29, Stevenson led by 854 votes out of nearly a million tabulated. The next day Johnson led by 693 votes. On the third day, tabulations showed Stevenson back in the lead, 119 votes ahead and only a few hundred votes uncounted. Two days later Johnson's votes were within 17 of Stevenson's total; and a week after the election, Johnson's total showed him ahead by 162 votes.

When Johnson went into the lead at the end of the week, Stevenson and some of his supporters went to Jim Wells County in South Texas to check on what they said were reports of padded ballot returns. They announced that in Box 13 of Jim Wells County 203 votes had been added after the balloting was supposed to end. They asked for a court order to change the Box 13 returns and wipe out the alleged irregularity. Johnson supporters promptly defended the returns in court and won an injunction forbidding any change in the Box 13 totals.

In a statewide broadcast, Johnson recalled the outcome of his Senate race in 1941 when corrections and changes days after election had wiped out his plurality. "All I want is justice. The accurate, official returns will show that I am the winner," he said.

Final authority in party primary election returns is the party itself, and the September convention of the Texas Democratic Party was only a week off. Both sides prepared to appear before the State Democratic Executive Committee when the time came to certify winners in the summer balloting. The convention site was Fort Worth, on September 14. The executive committee's crucial meeting was convened in the ballroom of the Blackstone Hotel on September 13. The only item on its agenda that would require more than five minutes' deliberation was the U. S. Senate nomination.

Chairman Robert W. Calvert (later Chief Justice of the Supreme Court of Texas) called the executive committee to order in the ballroom crowded with spectators, reporters and committee members. Secretary Vann M. Kennedy read the reports, a majority version and a minority version of the canvassing committee. The majority showed Johnson had received 494,191 votes, Coke Stevenson 494,104. The minority report had erased the returns from Box 13 in Jim Wells County.

Tension and excitement mounted in the crowded room as spokesmen for the two candidates argued their cases. Stevenson's supporters insisted that the votes from Box 13 be thrown out as fraudulent; Johnson's supporters wanted no change of the returns in any respect. Lyndon Johnson sat in the front row facing the committee, looking squarely and without change of expression at each speaker. Mr. Stevenson, smoking his pipe, sat a few feet away, watching intently. In the midst of booing, cat-calls, threats and challenges, the arguments finally ended and Chairman Calvert ordered the committee roll called.

Each district had two representatives with a vote apiece. By the time committee members from eighteen of the thirty-one districts had voted to throw out Box 13, it seemed certain that Johnson had lost. The vote stood 21 to 10 with less than half the districts remaining to be heard from. Then Tom Moore of Lockhart cast a pro-Johnson vote and others began to follow suit. Finally, the tally stood at 29 to 28 for Johnson and a few cheers went up. They died away when the chairman announced that Mrs. Seth Dorbandt of Conroe was changing her vote of "Aye" for Johnson and the majority report, to "Present." This made the tally 28 to 28. Chairman Calvert and Secretary Kennedy shuffled papers, inquired whether absentee members had come into the ballroom, looked at each other. Finally, Calvert raised his gavel to announce the tie vote, which if allowed to stand, meant a roll-call vote from the Convention's two thousand delegates the following day. This would be certain bedlam on the convention floor.

Suddenly a voice at the door of the ballroom called out, "Let me in—let me in!"

"Mr. Chairman, Mr. Chairman, I'm Charlie Gibson from Amarillo, and I vote 'Aye.' "

Chairman Calvert banged his gavel and announced the vote: 29 to 28 in favor of accepting the majority report. This gave Lyndon B. Johnson the senatorial nomination by 87 votes.

The crowd erupted into shouts and cheers and booing. Reporters on the scene called it a "madhouse."

Next day, the convention met in the Will Rogers auditorium across town. First battle to be fought centered on seating local delegations, the question being their stand on party loyalty and allegiance to the national ticket of Harry Truman and Alben Barkley. Center of this dispute were two rival delegations which had come to the convention, each claiming to be the official group from metropolitan Houston. One of them had refused to take a loyalty pledge. If it were

57

seated, there was a strong chance that the report on the senatorial election might be reversed on the floor of the convention.

A tense roll call of the convention resulted in the anti-Truman delegation's being ejected from the hall. The rest of the proceedings came quickly: pro-Truman loyalists named to key convention positions and a cheering ratification of the 87-vote victory of Lyndon B. Johnson as nominee for the U.S. Senate.

Lyndon and Mrs. Johnson sat in the front of the auditorium, watching the turmoil. When his nomination was approved and applauded, Johnson answered the chairman's invitation to speak by walking up the steps to the stage, standing quietly, and saying how much he appreciated the victory "after a hundred long days of campaigning." Johnson finished quickly with, "I intend to spend the next six years making Texas as good a United States Senator as I can possibly become."

The Stevenson forces were by no means finished with their attempt to upset the 87-vote verdict. They took evidence from Jim Wells County, including witnesses from Box 13, to federal court in Dallas. The judge ruled that they had proved their case. The Johnson forces appealed to the United States Supreme Court. Associate Justice Hugo Black issued an order that there was no federal jurisdiction in the contest. Johnson's name went on the general election ballot as the Democratic nominee. The Stevenson group made a final appeal to the United States Senate against the Johnson cause. The appeal was rejected.

Lyndon Johnson had not been accused of having any role personally in the Box 13 returns. The old controversy has been raked up often, however, and in gossip and political sloganeering has been laid as a charge against him. For years afterward, he allowed the talk to get under his skin. He still prefers almost any other subject to that one, though his reaction to it is no longer so strong as it once was.

The general election was an anticlimax. Johnson won by more than two to one, without a campaign.

After taking his oath, Senator Johnson told his staff: "Half of the voters of Texas didn't want me to be their Senator. Our job now is to prove to them that I can serve them well."

CHAPTER VIII

The twelve years of Lyndon Johnson's career in the United States Senate started quietly enough. He approached the dignified position of United States Senator from Texas with extreme care. He knew from his years in the House of Representatives and his wide experience in Washington that the Senate is like nothing else in our government. The Senators hold a sovereign status based on their representation of sovereign states. Their rules and customs reflect this; their attitudes express it.

His ingrained ability to sense the heart of a situation and to adapt himself correctly to its requirements came into public view at this time. His maturing process, during the next decade, turned out to be one of the nation's major political phenomena.

He set about learning everything there was to know about the Senate. Freed for the moment of the every-other-year election deadline that had faced him during his years in the House of Representatives, he had time for longer visits with colleagues and constituents, sometimes becoming almost voluble in conversations. This was a change from the brisk, rushing pace that had been his habit.

Johnson cultivated friendships among his colleagues, both because he is an innately friendly person and because an essential ingredient of an effective legislator is the ability to create and maintain pleasant relationships. He acquired restraint and decorum proper to his rank as a new Senator, a development that intrigued those who had known him when he was the high-strung, flamboyant Congressman from Austin.

He leaned with a new reliance on his old mentor, Sam Rayburn. Mr. Rayburn was re-elected Speaker of the House of Representatives at the same time Johnson started his Senate career. Far from interrupting their close relationship, the change in Johnson's position seemed to bring them closer.

Almost every afternoon about five o'clock a telephone rang in Johnson's office, and a gruff voice came through the instrument: "Tell Lyndon I'm waiting for him." The Speaker never deigned to give his name, and the secretaries never had to ask who was calling.

The call was the regular summons to Senator Johnson to join Speaker Rayburn and a few other senior members of

Congress in what they called "The Board of Education." This was a small office near Rayburn's own suite in the House wing of the Capitol. The "Board" met over a friendly glass to discuss backstage problems of the Congress—strategies, policies, individuals and tactics. The relaxed, informal conversations were much like the meetings of a football coaching staff planning the next game. Those daily conferences helped Lyndon Johnson to increase his knowledge of men and issues. They were lessons in the high art of politics.

Often, Senator Johnson would take the bachelor Speaker home for dinner. Here the conversations also centered on problems or ideas from their daily work.

Mrs. Johnson listened carefully and learned much about the workings of Congress. She also reinforced her admiration for her intensely dedicated husband's desire to do a superlative job as United States Senator.

The new junior Senator's constituents found him as accessible as he had been as a Congressman, and even more helpful. The extra prestige and authority of his position as Senator enabled him to serve them more effectively. He was receiving a new panorama of the variety of Texas problems from visitors and letters and telephone calls originating in all parts of the state. He was faced with the problem of mastering a far broader range of facts and circumstances than had confronted him as Congressman for the Tenth District.

The Senator expanded his office staff and worked it as long and as hard as usual. Mary Rather, his personal secretary in those days, remembers that he nearly always gave her a ride in his car to the office in the morning.

"He'd pick me up on Connecticut Avenue and by the time I sat down he was giving me instructions. I learned to keep my notebook outside my purse. By the time we reached the office he had outlined a whole day's work for me and had given me orders for the others that kept them jumping all day long, too."

Miss Rather said Johnson delegated duties to his staff members with wide latitude to get their assignments finished, but he also checked on their activities personally to be sure they were overlooking nothing.

He gave every staff member the feeling of being needed, of being important, of being responsible. It bred a loyalty to Johnson that some observers have said borders on the religious. Miss Rather says, "Once in a while I'd look up from my typewriter and ask myself whether I would work this hard for anybody else, including myself. I decided I wouldn't. . . ."

Back in Texas for a visit in 1951, the Johnsons solved a family problem and acquired the beginnings of the LBJ Ranch. The problem lay in the person of Mrs. Clarence Martin, widowed aunt of the Senator. She lived alone in the deteriorating old Johnson ranch house on the Pedernales, a few hundred yards from the cottage where Lyndon Johnson was born. She had found it necessary to sell off parcels of the land to meet her modest living needs. Senator Johnson offered her his family's former residence in Johnson City as a more comfortable, suitable dwelling, in exchange for what was left of the old "ranch" of 231 acres and the sagging house. She accepted the trade and the monthly expense check that went with it.

Lyndon and Lady Bird Johnson looked over their acquisition. The original stone portion, including the big room with a fireplace, was worth preserving, they decided. The frame additions needed replacing in large part. They set the work to going with the decision that they would live there after the rehabilitation was completed. They made the old place into a plain but comfortable residence. And the Senator bought a few cattle to graze on his land.

When Speaker Rayburn heard that Lyndon Johnson now had a "ranch" and some cattle, he said with feeling, "Thank the Lord, Lyndon will have something to talk about now besides business."

In the same year, Johnson accepted his first responsible job in the United States Senate, however, and soon he was talking "business," that is, Senate problems, at a greater rate than ever. He was chosen party Whip by the Senate Democrats.

It is the Whip's job to keep close contact with the Senators of his party, to determine their positions on legislation ahead of time and the reasons for their positions, to funnel into the hands of the party leader in the Senate every detail of the Senators' attitudes so that the leader could make effective decisions on Senate business.

Senator Johnson's abilities found new expression. His natural urge to be helpful to the party leader and to the individual Senators, and his inquisitive, retentive mind made him admirably suited to the job. The intimate knowledge of the national government entailed by this new responsibility was a big step to the qualifications that enabled him, nine years later, to serve the country well in the emergency of his sudden ascension to the presidency.

An additional duty undertaken at this time by Lyndon Johnson was chairmanship of a special Senate subcommittee to examine the war effort in Korea, the condition of our military and supply organizations, the contract procedures, and so on. He worked the subcommittee exhaustively. Their findings are credited with saving hundreds of millions of dollars in military procurement. What is best remembered in Congress about the Johnson subcommittee is that every one of the more than forty reports was unanimous. This was regarded as a remarkable testimony to Johnson's ability to bring partisans together in unity, regardless of party lines. Ordinarily, in a volume of reports of such scope, the minority, Democrats or Republicans, can find some point of disagreement, to criticize the majority's findings. Johnson's persuasive use of facts, his success in keeping his colleagues hard at their assignments, and his convincing sense of responsibility to the national interest above party considerations brought him new respect in the Senate.

As Senate Democratic Whip, too, Lyndon Johnson had a better vantage point from which to judge the coming turmoil in the national party as the Truman Administration went into its final decline. When 1952 brought the Democratic presidential nominating convention, Lyndon Johnson worked closely behind the scenes with Sam Rayburn, who as usual presided over that stormy meeting. Johnson and Rayburn managed to settle temporarily a contest by rival delegations coming up from Texas when they arranged for recognition to the group headed by Governor Allan Shivers. It was an effort on the part of Mr. Rayburn and Senator Johnson to patch up a party struggle back home between conservatives headed by the governor, and the liberals, who feared the others would not stay with the Democratic Party in the coming presidential race. The liberal prophecy came true in short order when the national party nominated Adlai Stevenson and the Republicans nominated Texas-born Dwight D. Eisenhower. When Adlai Stevenson said he disagreed with Texas' claim to own the tidelands along the Gulf Coast, and insisted the tidelands and the oil beneath them belonged to the nation, the Texas state hierarchy almost to a man officially supported the Republican candidate for President. They helped Mr. Eisenhower sweep the state into his electoral landslide over Mr. Stevenson.

Lyndon Johnson and Sam Rayburn supported Texas' claim to the tidelands but didn't find it necessary to abandon the Democratic nominee. Their efforts came to naught, however, against the phalanx of Texas Democrats-for-Eisenhower. Johnson and Rayburn already stood high in national party councils. Their rank rose there even though the national ticket failed. As chief Democrats in the Congress, they used their positions and moderate philosophies to exert deep influence on national events for the next eight years.

When the United States Congress convened in January, 1953, the Republicans had control of the House by a small margin and Speaker Rayburn gave way to Republican Speaker Joseph Martin. In the Senate, the Republicans numbered forty-eight; the Democrats forty-seven, and Senator Wayne Morse of Oregon, whose maverick status between the two parties made him unpredictable. The most influential Democrats in the Senate, headed by Walter George and Richard Russell of Georgia, settled on Lyndon Johnson as the man who should take the difficult role of party leader. He had been in the Senate five years, and was only forty-six years old. The confidence in him by Senators many years his senior in age and service was a remarkable recognition of Johnson's abilities. Lyndon Johnson leaned on them for advice, never lost an opportunity to assist them in every way his ingenuity could devise.

The close division in Congress in 1953–54 made it possible, if the Democratic leadership had been so minded, to tie the congressional process into hard knots. Senator Johnson as the new Democratic leader in the United States Senate, and Sam Rayburn as Democratic minority leader in the House, assessed this danger as the one to be avoided in the interest of national survival. They knew intimately the state of peril that existed in the world and knew that the United States Government, as the leader of the non-Communist nations, must not be weakened at the top by bitter partisan fighting.

Senator Johnson's concept of the role was not that he should wave a baton and shout, "Follow me," but rather that he should be the focal point where Democratic wisdom and experience were pooled and applied to the business of the Senate. His relationships with the Majority Leader, Senator Robert A. Taft of Ohio, were carefully correct as befitted the two party leaders in the Senate. Senator Taft took occasion more than once to compliment Senator Johnson on his fairness and honorable restraint in dealings with the Republican Administration.

A few months after being elevated to the leadership, Senator Johnson took time to visit in Texas. In city after city, he arranged small, intimate dinners for his principal supporters and told them how he was trying to perform. Even that soon, he had felt the needle of partisan critics, nationally and in Texas, who demanded that he lead daily attacks on the Republicans and their programs. Johnson discussed this criticism in order to point out his concept of responsibility. It did not include tearing up the governmental process merely for the sake of partisan victories.

There would be no advantage, he explained while they dined, to oppose simply for the sake of opposing. He mentioned the overwhelming popularity of the new President of the United States as evidenced by his electoral victory. Then Johnson used one of his favorite illustrations:

"If you're in an airplane flying somewhere, you don't run up to the cockpit and attack the pilot. Mr. Eisenhower is the only President we've got. We must help him when we can."

The following year, 1954, was the first opportunity in six years for Texas voters to register their judgment on Senator Lyndon Johnson. The only opponent who rose to challenge his re-election was Dudley Dougherty of Beeville, a wealthy young rancher. He waged a bitter campaign against Johnson, attacking in particular his record as a supporter of the Roosevelt-Truman international policies. Johnson had measured sentiment in Texas with his usual accuracy and decided that Dougherty, a newcomer to politics, wouldn't attract much support. The Senator did not put on a speaking campaign on his own behalf, but rather relied on his friends and supporters to carry the appeal for his re-election. The result was an overwhelming victory for Johnson. It cleared the records, his friends felt, of the last vestige of his narrow 87-vote victory of six years before.

In the general elections of 1954, the hairline margin between Democrat and Republican membership in the Senate was maintained but reversed. There were forty-eight Democrats, plus Senator Morse when he felt like voting with them; there were forty-seven Republicans. In the House, Democrats had a slightly larger majority, 232 to 203. Johnson and Rayburn felt that the return of their party to a majority position, however thin the edge, showed that the voters appreciated their policy of moderation.

The year was historic, too, in its last half as the setting for a virtuoso performance by Democratic Leader Johnson as the United States Senate went about the business of censuring one of its members, Senator Joseph R. McCarthy, Republican of Wisconsin. The motion for censure was offered in the summer of 1954 after the Wisconsin maverick had set the Senate—and the nation—into an uproar with his one-man attacks on personages and agencies of the national government.

Not only was Senator McCarthy noisy in and out of the Senate as he repeated his charges of Communist conspiracies in high places, but the ultra-conservatives who espoused his views flooded the mails with letters and leaflets supporting him. His Roman Catholic background also was considered to give him political potency in important vote-heavy areas of the nation. It was with much reluctance that his colleagues in the Senate approached the matter of clipping his wings. Only twice before in 171 years had the Senate of the United States censured one of its members, and neither case was comparable to McCarthy's in political explosiveness. But a fellow-Republican, Senator Ralph Flanders of Vermont, climaxed his months-long criticisms of Senator McCarthy by introducing Senate Resolution 301 on July 30 to censure McCarthy for contempt of the Senate.

Democratic Leader Johnson worked closely with the Republican leader, Senator William Knowland, to have the censure resolution referred to a select committee of three Republicans and three Democrats, men of notably judicial temperaments. This was done on August 6 and the select committee went to work investigating the charges leveled by Senator Flanders. The inquiry went on into the autumn. After the November elections, the Senate reconvened to consider the select committee's recommendations.

Here began the series of votes on those recommendations that stamped Lyndon Johnson as a leader of his party par excellence. The Democrats voted together in rare harmony on every test while the Republican members of the Senate divided almost half-and-half. The final vote to "condemn" the conduct of Senator McCarthy came on a roll call in which all 44 Democrats, the lone Independent and 22 Republicans said "aye" and 22 other Republicans said "nay".

The Republican administration took the public credit for downgrading its senatorial gadfly but the senators knew who assured, by his canny and expert leadership, the solid Democratic majority that made the action decisive. It was Senator Lyndon B. Johnson of Texas.

Thus secured in his top position and freshly re-elected to a new six-year term in the Senate, Lyndon Johnson publicly outlined his views on issues the Democrats intended to press: ". . . We will proceed as rapidly as possible to build up the nation's defenses; to assure our farmers a fairer share of the nation's income, to break the bottlenecks of foreign trade; to broaden the credit base and put an end to the evil effects of the hard-money policy. . . ." Then he added: ". . . we Democrats will cooperate with the President on any measure which our inner consciences tell us will advance the best interests of the country. But in any event, there will be no personal attacks upon the integrity of the President or upon his intentions."

The end of the Korean conflict opened the way for Congress to resume approval to public works expenditures: dams, harbor and channel improvements and other water management programs. Lyndon Johnson was among the first to move in this field. He knew intimately the list of Texas water conservation projects which had been put on the congressional shelf when the war in Asia broke out.

"I want us to start at least one new dam in Texas every year from now on," he told his staff. This is a target he hit squarely during his remaining eight years in the Senate.

Majority Leader Johnson threw himself into the congressional session of 1955 with more zest than ever. Sure of himself and totally steeped in detailed knowledge about his colleagues, he personally touched every particle of Senate business. His days started at dawn, ended late in most evenings. He worked on Saturdays and always visited the office Sunday. He interested himself in all the problems of the other Senators, exerted his own efforts to help them serve their constituents in all the useful ways, large and small, that United States Senators affect the lives of the people back home. Johnson, of course, did not neglect his own constituents from Texas, but his concept of the role of majority leader included a sense of responsibility to the constituents of all his Democratic colleagues. Because of his unceasing attention to his colleagues' work, and his skill in persuasive argument on matters he considered ready for action, Lyndon Johnson usually could muster a convincing majority for legislation. Considering the one- or two-vote party-line division in the Senate, these majorities appeared to observers to border on miraculous. Few persons outside the Senate knew the combination of persuasion, leadership and detailed maneuvering that Johnson exerted to his fellow Senators. Nor could they know how he read and talked and listened, how he judged timing and personalities and issues to bring about the combination that produced results.

Lyndon Johnson as Majority Leader was a study in applied urgency. Within the careful limits of senatorial courtesy, he managed to hustle the work along, and so intent was he on accomplishing the maximum that he thought of nothing else from January to June.

No matter how long or arduous had been his day, a messenger brought to his bedroom each evening a fat package of memoranda, mail to be signed, and other items that his hard-working staff knew he would want to look at. When he went to bed, he kept this packet within arm's reach. He is a light and restless sleeper. Sometime after midnight, he would awaken and reach for the bundle of paperwork. As often as not, something in the stack would stir him to telephone an assistant, perhaps at 2 A.M. or 4 A.M., and issue instructions on a subject that might range from National Security concerns to a constituent's problem or some other of the thousand varieties of interest in which Johnson stayed constantly active.

Lyndon Johnson's urge to communicate is overpowering. It led him as a freshman Congressman to set a rule that his staff has lived by ever since—every letter must be answered the day it is received. This burden of work, six hundred or more letters a day, day after day, year after year, and often many more than six hundred, added other refinements. Copies of Johnson's speeches went to whichever mailing list was appropriate. Excerpts from the *Congressional Record* on matters of interest to one constituent or many constituents were sent out by his staff. The same urge to communicate, which of course invites communicators, was responsible for an intricate battery of telephone lines in Johnson's numerous offices. Even more spectacularly, he equipped all his automobiles, official and private, with radio telephones so that he could get in touch with anybody, anywhere, any time. This was hard on the hired help but it kept Johnson's tireless energy and insatiable curiosity perking at full speed.

He often ended a day by taking a few staff members and maybe an out-of-town visitor home for a quick refresher before going out to a late dinner and dancing interlude. While everybody else was chatting and sipping, Johnson would sit under a floor lamp signing mail with a quick scrawl, rapidly reading staff memos, raising his head from time to time for a brief comment on the papers in front of him or on a bit of conversation in the room. When the foot-high stack of mail and memoranda had been winnowed, he was ready to go dining and dancing until past midnight.

The strain finally began to make itself felt. Toward the end of June, 1955, he noticed that he felt continuously tired. His old friend Sam Rayburn upbraided him one evening about overdoing his work and not taking proper care of himself. Johnson promised that when the session ended, which he hoped might be in another two months, he was going to the LBJ Ranch in Texas and take it easy for the remainder of the year. In the meantime, he planned a holiday week end with George and Herman Brown at their estate near Middleburg, Virginia.

Preparing to take the unaccustomed two days off, Johnson worked late at his office on Saturday, July 2, outlining the Senate calendar for the coming week. He was irritable, according to the newspaper reporters who talked to him during a press conference that afternoon. Weariness showed in his face and posture.

Finally, he left the Capitol, entered his waiting limousine, and told the chauffeur to start for Virginia. As they rolled along through the humid evening, Johnson began having trouble drawing his breath. He opened the windows of the air-conditioned car but that didn't relieve his gasping. By the time he reached the Browns' residence, he thought he was in the throes of a digestive upset. His hosts summoned a local physician, who looked at the Senator and said his symptoms might be those of a heart illness.

"If you think it may be a heart attack, let's act like it is a heart attack," said Johnson. He began to give orders about an ambulance, about calling his closest, most trusted assistant, Walter Jenkins, to meet him at the hospital. After a brief and detailed conversation with Jenkins there, Johnson went into shock.

A team of naval physicians took over. With oxygen and drugs, they pulled him through the crisis period during the night. They pronounced his illness a myocardial infarction, moderately severe. And they said that for the next several months he was finished with anything except complete rest.

In the weeks at the hospital, with Mrs. Johnson at his side day and night, and his two daughters coming in for daily visits, Johnson began a period of recovery and introspection.

The quick outpouring of expressions of concern for his health came from all parts of the capital and throughout the nation. President Eisenhower and Vice President Nixon, his colleagues in the Senate, friends in and out of government, Texans and citizens of all other states made known their admiration for Lyndon Johnson and their wishes for his recovery.

Hundreds of editorials praised his work in the Senate. Lyndon Johnson discovered that he was a national figure of first rank.

From the hospital room, he issued a statement giving the United States Senate the major credit for the applause that was coming to him. He called attention to the volume of work accomplished, to the major foreign and domestic policies advanced by the Senate, to the lack of bitter partisan quarreling, and to the independence of the Congress in its relations with the executive branch. The statement, he felt, fully answered those who, before his illness, had accused him of weakening the Democratic Party by cooperating too closely with President Eisenhower. His perusal of his mail in the hospital convinced him that his policy of moderation and responsibility matched the mood of a majority of the American people. His statement about the session of Congress just ending concluded:

"The President's recommendations were considered thoroughly and examined from the standpoint of how they fitted into the needs of the country. In many cases they were improved; in some they were passed practically without change; others were not acted upon at all. In short, Congress . . . discharged its constitutional obligation of representing the American people. . . ."

Then Lyndon Johnson went to the LBJ Ranch to complete his convalescence. Typically, he set out to do more to safeguard his health than his physicians recommended. He ate less even than they prescribed—until Mrs. Johnson ordered him to follow the official caloric count. He reduced his weight from 220 to 179, six pounds less than prescribed. He had smoked three packs of cigarettes a day for years but he had his last one in the ambulance going to the hospital. Now he chewed gum, sucked on low-calorie candies, and resolutely faced up to the "no smoking" order. He kept a package of cigarettes beside his bed to test his will power. He met the test. Today, incidentally, he is almost a rabid anti-cigarette missionary among his friends.

But above all, Lyndon Johnson rested and read and thought deeply about all the things he'd been too busy to remember all those years in Washington.

The drastic change of pace forced on him by the heart attack gave Senator Johnson the new experience of reflection without immediate action. Always before this period, thought and action occurred for him almost simultaneously. He never again was as impatient or as impetuous, although his capacity for swift decisions hasn't been reduced. He perfected to an important degree during his convalescence the probing talent of his mind that so many associates have called "the most active I've ever known." The total effect of his restful autumn on the banks of the Pedernales was a permanent upturn in the combining in Lyndon Johnson of deep wisdom with his urge to produce active results.

He read Plato and Jefferson as well as contemporary writings on politics and government. He reviewed and sorted out all the aspects of his national role, and turned over in his mind ideas for improving himself as a Senator and as a national party leader. He lay in the sun and became Indian-brown.

During that autumn famous visitors visited in a steady procession—Adlai Stevenson, Sam Rayburn, Estes Kefauver, Arthur Godfrey. They found a calm and relaxed Lyndon Johnson, and marveled at the change even more than at his rapid recovery.

Receiving a visitor, Johnson lay in a reclining chair, a low-calorie soft drink by his elbow. Soft music came from a sound system recently installed in the ranch house. Two secretaries with desks just inside the veranda tapped their typewriters, still answering the flow of letters and messages that hadn't stopped coming. At his call, one of them would bring the albums of photographs and telegrams which Mrs. Johnson had compiled from the mountain of mail and the visits of famous personages during his illness. The Senator took visible pride in showing these. He discussed his medical history in detail, and showed his latest electrocardiograph reading. He talked about the recent session of Congress and its intricacies. He talked about the need for rain in the neighborhood and the prospects for deer hunting in late autumn. His voice was soft and his manner reflective.

As strength and vigor returned, Lyndon Johnson thought more each day about the presidential election year just ahead, the challenges it would bring, and the opportunities.

CHAPTER IX

Lyndon Johnson's complete recovery from his heart ailment became evident in the way he surmounted a series of challenging events during the 1956 presidential election year.

Resuming his duties as Majority Leader of the Senate, he continued to give close personal attention to the work of his colleagues. He did pace himself more sensibly. He took rest periods, stayed rigidly on his diet, and turned over to his staff, more seasoned now, many of the chores he previously handled himself. He enjoyed a new sense of sureness in his position and responsibilities.

Congress was preparing for the summer conventions that would start the presidential campaign. With Democrats ruling both houses and a Republican in the White House, the sparring for advantage did not add any speed to the pace of legislation. Moreover, the two legislative leaders had a problem back home in Texas.

Mr. Rayburn directed the party faithful in Texas to arrange for a delegation to the national convention pledged to support Lyndon Johnson as favorite-son nominee for President, and elect Johnson chairman of the delegation. Mr. Rayburn had no illusions about an actual Johnson nomination but the effort would enhance Texas' party prestige. This was to be done through the customary stepladder of local precinct conventions, followed by county conventions and climaxed at the state convention.

Governor Allan Shivers, head of the 1952 Democrats for Eisenhower, was in his final year as governor in 1956. He decided that his position called for him to contest the Rayburn-Johnson forces at the precinct level to determine if the traditional Democrats of the state wanted him instead of Johnson to head their national convention delegation. He began to make speeches urging that his own leadership be accepted. This attempt to wrest the control of the party from Rayburn and Johnson had some chances for success because Mr. Eisenhower was still popular in Texas, and Governor Shivers naturally had closer contacts with more Texans than did Sam Rayburn or Lyndon Johnson. The Senator found it necessary to come home and visit strategic communities to whip up party sentiment on his behalf. But he made only one statewide address, a fatherly talk on television. He knew his listeners had a strong Democratic tradition in their blood regardless of how much they liked Ike. Johnson told Texas Democrats that the "Republicans and the radicals are trying to destroy the Democratic Party in Texas and leave it to the hotheads." He recalled that less than a year earlier Governor Shivers had called Johnson an acceptable possibility for President. "Yet when Sam Rayburn agreed with him this spring, he picked up his marbles and went home."

It was Johnson's first TV effort. It was effective. When the precinct conventions met across Texas, a resounding majority of them endorsed the Senator both as chairman of the state delegation to Chicago and as favorite-son nominee for President. The results of this grass-roots test made Lyndon Johnson smile with satisfaction.

His old friend and former assistant, John B. Connally, made the nominating speech to the national convention, urging Lyndon Johnson for President. It was a brief episode, for the delegates promptly renominated Adlai Stevenson as their choice.

As chairman of the Texas delegation, Lyndon Johnson watched the ensuing dramatic contest for the vice presidential nomination. Senator John Kennedy of Massachusetts and Senator Estes Kefauver locked in a close race for the honor. At the last moment, Johnson swung the Texas votes into Kennedy's column. It wasn't enough to win for him, but the young Senator remembered Johnson's act, and it helped set the stage for what happened to both of them four years later.

When Stevenson suffered an even more crushing defeat at the hands of President Eisenhower that autumn, the liberal wing of the Democratic Party began a barrage of criticism aimed at Lyndon Johnson and Sam Rayburn. The liberal spokesmen said and wrote that the moderate stance of the two Texans had cost Stevenson any chance to win because of failure in Congress to dramatize liberal issues and programs.

The unrest over the Rayburn-Johnson team started in Texas even before the November elections. The state convention of Texas Democrats met at Forth Worth to certify party nominees chosen during the summer primary elections. Price Daniel had won a close race for governor and was supposed to be certified. But a block of vocal liberal delegations threatened to seize control of the convention and nullify Daniel's ballot victory. Whether they could have succeeded or not is open to question. They did not get the chance to try because Lyndon Johnson held the convention machinery under tight rein. In a series of ruthless backstage maneuvers, Johnson so managed the credential committee's decisions that most of the revolt-minded liberals were not even allowed to take part in the convention. It was what Johnson sternly called a "lesson in political integrity."

What the episode meant in the career of Lyndon Johnson was worth noting: in the spring, he had defeated the conservative wing of Texas Democrats, and in the fall he had frustrated the liberal wing. It demonstrated that Johnson not only liked the middle of the political road—the prudent, responsible posture he believed most citizens endorsed—but that he could fight and win to stay in the middle of the road under challenges from either side.

The turmoil of this political year put him under repeated stresses. He seemed to thrive under them, however, and his energy now approached its pre-coronary pitch.

Late in the year Johnson sought relaxation at the LBJ Ranch. He occasionally went deer hunting, his favorite outdoor sport. Watching him run up a knoll to see whether a shot had downed a buck, one of Johnson's companions shook his head in wonderment: "Can you believe he's the man who almost died of a heart attack summer before last?" When he wasn't carrying a rifle, Johnson drove through the bushy pastures, counting deer and watching them run at his approach. He would shout with exuberance at the sight.

One afternoon he paced back and forth along the bank of the Pedernales near the ranch house, talking to a friend about political battles and his future. He mused aloud about the criticisms of his moderate policies printed in Northern and Eastern journals, and spoken in meetings of national liberal Democrats. These grated on his sensitive nature. Was he smart, he wondered, to stay in politics, work eighteen hours a day, and put up with sniping from those who disagreed with him? He reviewed his economic situation. Mrs. Johnson's broadcasting company, now a television as well as a radio concern, was thriving. A major airline had offered Johnson its presidency at $100,000 a year. Should he get out of politics and accept? He momentarily relished the idea of taking over a corporate enterprise that needed a leader. But politics?

The next remark answered the question. Johnson remembered his smashing precinct convention victory the previous spring. He'd taught the conservatives how to play the game, he said with a snort. "But you know, I like that fellow Shivers. He's tough. He'll grab the flag and take his folks somewhere. I like that in a leader."

73

Johnson said no more about quitting politics. He soon began talking of the coming session of Congress. "We're going to pass a civil rights bill next summer, something the liberals are yelling for, and I bet they'll find something to criticize about that, too."

Before that month ended, the National Democratic Committee created a Democratic Advisory Council which would, it was said, formulate legislative policies for Democrats. It was a deliberate slap at Speaker Rayburn and Majority Leader Johnson. They treated it with cold disdain. They insisted that they were elected to office, and were elected to their congressional leadership positions by duly chosen representatives of the people. They, not a political committee, would continue to set legislative goals for the Democrats. But the unpleasantness of this party struggle, and the fact that newspapers and some magazines made much of it, fed Johnson's discontent. He took satisfaction from the fact that most Democratic Senators took strong issues with the advisory council and told it to mind its own business.

In the ensuing session of Congress, Johnson's prophecy about a civil rights bill proved correct. The skill he showed in steering through the United States Senate the first civil rights bill to be voted by that body in eighty-seven years brought him new admiration. The right of unlimited debate in the Senate has enabled members to talk a measure to death when they are determined enough in their opposition. This had been the fate of anti-lynching bills and other attempts in the past to write federal legislation in the field of civil rights. The Southern Senators could be counted on to talk against such bills until their sponsors abandoned them in the interest of getting on to some other order of business.

The Senate debated the 1957 Civil Rights Bill for two weeks in July. Its provisions dealt with guarantees of the right to vote, a thorny issue in some Southern states where trick laws and tough administration barred Negroes from the polls. The most controversial part of the bill was called Title III, designed to give the U. S. Attorney General new and almost unlimited powers to cut across traditional jurisprudence in enforcing the right to vote. Johnson's most trusted advisers, among them Dean Acheson and Clark Clifford, two Truman Administration stalwarts still prominent in Washington, convinced him that Title III was unwise and indefensible. The Majority Leader maneuvered the Senate into voting on that provision first. The Senators struck it out. Then he marshaled them to vote on the Civil Rights Bill. They passed it. Johnson's other prophecy then came true.

The liberals castigated him for the elimination of Title III.

In October, 1957, the first Sputnik went into orbit and the public clamor over the American missile program broke into full cry. When the second Sputnik went up, and the first American launching effort fizzled in front of the news cameras, public criticism reached a crescendo. Nobody in authority responded affirmatively until Senator Johnson called a series of public hearings to be conducted by the watchdog subcommittee of the Senate Armed Services Committee.

Johnson's subcommittee had looked askance earlier at some aspects of the defense establishment, but without finding much to report, and without stirring much public interest in their work. This time the atmosphere was entirely different. Johnson caught the public mood and characteristically exemplified it.

He galvanized the subcommittee's staff, reinforced it with new talent, and with his colleagues zeroed in on the missile program.

The day following the launching of the second Soviet satellite, Johnson and two of his colleagues spent seven hours in the Pentagon being briefed on the status of United States space efforts. When, in the course of this day-long discussion, it developed that there was no explanation for the fact that a crucial decision in missile development and production had been deferred from July to October and then had not been made at all, Johnson said with asperity, "Gentlemen, you'll be seeing a lot more of my committee and my staff. You need a good deal of help."

In the crowded committee room where the hearings unfolded in day and night sessions, with only a brief recess for Christmas, Johnson and his fellow Senators probed and pried, examined and cross-examined. They quizzed generals and admirals and civilian experts on every detail of the nation's sprawled-out efforts to get a space program going. They uncovered for the taxpayers' contemplation a pattern of cross-purposes overlaid with red tape, and labyrinthine channels in which scientists and technical experts wandered in frustrated despair.

Johnson led most of the grilling. He did not temper his sharp, impatient questions to military rank or executive position. It was an ordeal he did not relish. Occasionally he would turn the gavel over to Senator Symington or one of the other members and slip away to the Senate health club for a massage. In the late evenings, he sometimes took a few friends out for dinner and a little dancing. It never took his mind off the hearings, however. Between trips around the dance floor he talked only of the investigation and its significance.

So well had Johnson and his staff prepared themselves for the investigation that the Majority Leader could keep it to factual questions, away from weakening overtones of political partisanship. Johnson was careful to do this. He realized that any benefit to the country from the hearings would be rubbed out if politics overshadowed the troubles of the missile effort.

Largely as a result of the pressure applied by Johnson, the administration found ways to speed up and coordinate the complicated missile program. Most of the top personnel directly involved said later that Lyndon Johnson contributed more than any other one man in the government to the development of the American space program.

The final three years of Johnson's leadership in the Senate brought him national recognition on a scale he had not known before. By this time it was an established fact of Washington life that Majority Leader Johnson held in his big hands most of the answers to the fate of legislation, regardless of its origin. He knew exactly how each Senator would react on every issue. He was usually able to arrange the Senate calendar so that no piece of business which really required action was delayed. By personal example, he nurtured the bipartisan support for President Eisenhower on international policies which, Johnson felt, would strengthen the position of the United States in world affairs.

Lyndon Johnson's mother, Rebekah Baines Johnson, died in September, 1958. A long illness prevented her from being in her son's company as often as she wanted to be. During the final year of her life, Johnson made flying trips to her bedside in Austin, usually without any public announcement or notice. The close bond between mother and son had grown closer through the years; he had long since enshrined the memory of Sam Johnson, but in the twenty years of Mrs. Johnson's widowhood, her son Lyndon had been her mainstay, and she, to an important degree, his. Her loss was a major sorrow.

His parents remain much in Johnson's consciousness today. He finds occasion, in conversation or in acknowledging a public introduction, to say that "Only my mother ever thought I'd get as far as I did. . . ." or to make a reference to his father's political aphorisms.

Beginning in 1956, the series of river projects which he shepherded through Congress year after year on behalf of his home state began to materialize in the form of new dams.

The Majority Leader never turned down an invitation to dedication ceremonies or other formal recognition of the progress of these works. Throughout his twelve years in the Senate, he preached the gospel of water conservation, flood prevention and cheaper electric power that had been his theme song as a young Congressman. He knew the grim statistics of every river in Texas—how many persons perished in floodtime, how many dollars' worth of damage the untamed streams inflicted on towns and countryside. And he knew the other statistics, too: the dollar value of water to farms and ranches, the economic stimulus of reservoirs to nearby communities, the growing outdoor recreation trend, and the need of Texas' burgeoning cities for adequate water supplies in the future. These factors he wove into speeches and private conversation. He put the spurs to Texas officialdom to start at long last on a state water program, and he welcomed Texas delegations to Washington any time they wanted to talk with him about managing water.

Visitors to Johnson's offices during this period had a new story to tell nearly every time they went home. His multiplying duties and responsibilities allowed Johnson to spread out from the Senate office building in a big way. He redecorated the Majority Leader's large suite off the Senate floor in regal green and gold, creating an atmosphere of quiet luxury in keeping with his rank. These sophisticated surroundings were a great contrast to his original office in Washington in 1931; they were, in a sense, symbolic of the development of the man himself from rambunctious congressional assistant to master politician. There was, however, no slackening of the Johnson pace. The room where he sat was large, high-ceilinged, with crystal and metal ornaments. The piled-up desk was cleared off twice a day but never stayed that way long.

Johnson stayed nearly always in the Capitol, close to the Senate, but his telephone system gave instant communication to the increasing number of staff persons who activated his orders on a widening front. He held the top positions in the Senate's Democratic ranks. He was chairman of the Democratic caucus, chairman of the Democratic policy committee, held in his hands every line of party responsibility. The fact that his colleagues entrusted to one man all the duties usually spread among four or five Senators is perhaps the highest tribute to Johnson's abilities on record. All these duties he took on eagerly, and still remained active on the appropriations committee and the watchdog subcommittee of armed services.

Close observers of the Senate scene found Johnson's regime a constant fascination. "He runs the Senate like a caged tiger. . . ." one reporter wrote. "When he steps into the Senate chamber, Lyndon Johnson walks with the assurance of a Bavarian landgrave stepping into his castle," another account began. "Sitting slumped in his aisle seat, he can sense everything that is going on behind him without turning around. . . . Johnson has worked and suffered to achieve his domination. . . ."

As Johnson added party authority to his Senate leadership, a few Senators began to call for more voice in the caucuses and the policy committee proceedings. Sympathetic reporters picked up this theme. One of them wrote that the Democrats of the Senate were beginning to tire of Johnson's holding them together. The Majority Leader put it to a vote. By a division of fifty-one for Johnson, twelve for a loosening of his authority, the issue was settled. It became apparent then that seven years of what some called Johnson's "iron rule" had not damaged the egos or the prerogatives of the majority of the Senate.

The Majority Leader had by that time perfected to an absolute instrument his knowledge of what every Senator would do on all official occasions. Before major votes, Johnson had in his hand a tally sheet showing the probable outcome. Almost always, the final result matched his calculations exactly.

When he could find the time, Senator Johnson enjoyed informal conversations in his office with visiting personages and a few veteran journalists. Often at the height of his Senate power the visitors wanted to sound Johnson out on his future. Naturally, they'd work the conversation around to the prospects, pro and con, of his ever becoming President of the United States. Johnson's invariable reply before 1960 dwelt on the fact that no Southerner had been elected President since the Civil War, that he was satisfied to be a member of the United States Senate, the greatest deliberative body in the world, that he really was just a fellow from the banks of the Pedernales and he wasn't convinced he had all the qualifications a President needed.

For Lyndon Johnson viewed the office of President of the United States with awe and reverence. He had watched at close range three Presidents. As Majority Leader, he sat often with President Eisenhower on legislative questions that crossed party lines. Johnson's concept of the heavy, almost crushing responsibilities of the presidency tempered his instinctive urge to seek its power for himself. And he was not able to detect and predict the cross-currents of national political sentiment with the same sure finesse he used on the Senate. This factor made his natural caution keener in those days of 1958 and 1959 when Lyndon Johnson was being called "the second most powerful man in the country." He realized that in spite of his prominence in Washington, he had not made an impact on the great body of citizens outside of Texas.

There, Lyndon Johnson left nothing to chance.

With a foresight and a caution that are basic to his character, Johnson weighed the rising possibility that he (1) might try for the 1960 Democratic nomination as he was being urged to do by many of his long-time political associates; (2) might be defeated and thus lose his position in the Senate, since his term was to expire in 1960; (3) might find a way to seek re-election to the Senate while also being available as a possible presidential nominee.

To his friends in Texas, notably his ally, Governor Price Daniel, Johnson presented the complicated problem. Their solution in the state legislative session of 1959 was to rewrite the Texas election code. The new law changed the time of party primaries from July and August to May and June. This would permit Johnson to be renominated as Senator before the national political conventions in July. It also would answer long-standing complaints in Texas that July and August are too warm for sensible politicking. The code also provided, as rewritten, that a candidate's name could appear on the ballot in two places, meaning of course that if Senator Johnson were to be on the national presidential ticket, he could also be offered as United States Senator for re-election. His friends felt this was a prudent way to protect their most prominent political figure.

This change in Texas' election code to accommodate a next-year presidential situation had a precedent. In 1951 the code was amended to permit cross-filing so that, a year later, a state official could run on both party tickets. It was known then as the Eisenhower law.

Johnson accepted speaking engagements in the autumn of 1959 that carried him to all parts of the state, by plane, by helicopter, by automobile. He appeared before big-city leaders, professional groups, small-town crowds and the rural people who had always understood him best.

Enthusiastic LBJ supporters usually succeeded, in the wake of his personal appearances, in organizing Johnson-for-President clubs in their communities.

At Bastrop, in the heart of the old Tenth District where

he had started his congressional career, a band of Johnson friends gathered several thousand Rural Electric Cooperative members from over the entire district for a fish fry and speech by the Senator. To usher him before the microphone outside the community hall, they staged a convention-style parade with banners and snake-dancing lines of "delegates" yelling and stomping for Lyndon B. Johnson. He watched the floodlighted crowd impassively, then stood up to acknowledge the ovation. In a drawling voice, he advised them that "We have to take this thing one step at a time. There's a lot of work to do in the Senate. We'll just go one step at a time." But he obviously enjoyed the excitement and back-slapping of the evening.

A different sort of gathering gave the Johnson bandwagon a push at the plush ranch of an oil millionaire near Austin. About a thousand guests came from all over Texas, in airplanes, limousines and lesser conveyances. There was a separate food line for the airplane pilots. The host reported later that one man flew to the ranch in a single-engine plane, and counted sixty-two twin-motored planes parked around the airstrip; embarrassed, he flew on to Austin and was driven to the party in a taxicab. The crowd pitched into the problem of financing a Johnson-for-President campaign and helped to solve it.

In the speeches he made during this time, most of them extemporaneous and informal, Johnson used the language of an article he had written a year before for *Harper's* entitled, "My Political Philosophy":

"I am a free man, an American, a United States Senator, and a Democrat, in that order. I am also a liberal, a conservative, a Texan, a taxpayer, a rancher, a businessman, a consumer. . . ."

He resisted the idea that he could be called a Southern Democrat, or a Liberal Democrat, or a Conservative Democrat. He was, he insisted, a Democrat—period. His belief in the Democratic Party as the instrument through which the people could manage their government better admitted of no prefixes.

Johnson also took frequent occasion to assail the "nit-pickers, the prevaricators, the slanderers, the dividers who would split the country. I regard the division of the people as the work of weak men—of little men—too weak to lead the strength of a people united. . . ."

Through most of his public utterances ran the thread of his belief in strong military power to back up national policy, and his belief that the President ought to have utmost freedom to use his power without sharpshooting from Congress on questions of international relationships. He told his Texas audiences what Nikita Khrushchev had said when the Soviet premier had been introduced to Johnson in Washington: "I know all about you. I have read all your speeches and I don't like any of them."

Johnson's national stature also caused him to be invited to New York, to Des Moines, and other cities for occasional speeches and Democratic meetings. He used these opportunities to talk about the need for helping poorer nations to feed themselves, to get capital for development—he suggested a Liberty Bank for long-term, low-cost loans to struggling, emerging countries.

In October of 1959, Senator and Mrs. Johnson entertained the president of Mexico, Adolfo Lopez Mateos, at their LBJ Ranch in the first spectacle of its kind ever seen in the hill country. It was to become later an almost familiar scene of international gatherings with all the Western trimmings. When President Lopez Mateos arrived, he came with Senator Johnson in a helicopter, stepped out on a red carpet to the music of a Mexican band. Sam Rayburn and Harry Truman followed in a smaller helicopter. There were eight hundred guests, gathered from all over Texas, at the Johnsons' invitation to eat barbecued steaks and listen to speeches of mutual admiration from the guests of honor and the host. A sign, prominently hung in one of the trees of the grove where the feast was held, proclaimed: *Lyndon Johnson sera presidente.* It was the first public indication that Mr. Rayburn and Mr. Truman were winning their persuasive argument that Johnson owed it to the Democratic Party to make a try for the presidential nomination in 1960. Nobody at the ranch that day dissented, but Lyndon Johnson still had inner doubts and questions to ask himself before he actually began a serious effort to seek the party's highest honor.

Mr. Rayburn had taken some preliminary steps on behalf of a Johnson presidential nomination campaign. He caused an office to be opened in Washington to compile lists of political figures—large and small—who might be favorable. He passed the word among well-heeled Johnson admirers that if they wanted their favorite to be in the running in 1960, their money could help pay for campaign expenses. He enlisted John B. Connally to become director of a Johnson campaign, if and when.

Mrs. Johnson, looking to a role she could foresee for herself if her husband hit the trail for the presidential nomination, took a course in public speaking that winter. She also enlisted the designers at Dallas' famous Neiman-Marcus department store to turn out a "Ladies for Lyndon" uniform. This colorful red, white and blue ensemble could be furnished to feminine Johnson fans for $27.80.

Still, Johnson, the master strategist, watched and waited and analyzed the political scene without saying, even to his associates, whether he actually would try for the nomination in Los Angeles in the coming summer.

CHAPTER X

From his position of political eminence in Washington as 1960 began, Lyndon B. Johnson watched the center of Democratic presidential aspirations coalesce around the Senate. His own chances furnished constant conversational material for others while he kept silent. Senator John F. Kennedy of Massachusetts zestfully built up his professional organization to search out delegate strength across the country. Senator Stuart Symington of Missouri had admirers in the Middle West and East, and figured in all the speculative calculations of the political reporters. Senator Hubert Humphrey of Minnesota, articulate and impeccably liberal, seemed to be in a fairly good position to attract support if there was to be a real convention contest. Humphrey, however, sought to advance the cause of Adlai Stevenson more than he did his own.

By the end of April, Lyndon Johnson had guided another civil rights bill, after fifty-three days of debate and maneuvering, through the Senate to strengthen the voting safeguards of the 1957 version. His own voting record since 1937 in House and Senate was being combed by political analysts to determine how he compared with other possible Democratic presidential timbre. It was a record essentially liberal, the compilations showed, though not doctrinaire liberal; and not nearly so liberal as the voting stands of Senators Kennedy, Humphrey and Symington.

Johnson's well-wishers pointed to the unquestioned fact that he had avoided demagoguery throughout his political career. They showed that he had supported the causes of stronger military defense, welfare spending, public works, liberal farm-support prices, aid to education, foreign aid, mutual security, reciprocal trade, the United Nations, and better relations with the peoples of Central and South America. His stands on taxation, on regulation of labor unions, and especially on reducing the spending requests of the Eisenhower Administration, they said, should make him acceptable to the business community. His record since he became a leader in the Senate had veered away from the Southern overtones that marked it prior to 1955, the analysis continued. Johson had a national and a world outlook that eminently qualified him to be a candidate for President.

Johnson himself didn't question this analysis of his growth

and breadth, but he still weighed his concepts of the presidency against his own and his colleagues' abilities. A close friend was quoted as saying, at this stage of 1960, "He knows he's got a heart big enough to be President. He knows he's got guts enough to be President, but he wonders whether he has intelligence and ability enough to be President—and wonders if any man does. He's seen them all—those who have had it and those who are trying for the job. To his mind none of them are big enough."

The Majority Leader knew full well, too, that he was plainly and eminently a Texan in the minds of all who knew him. He knew his Southern drawl didn't sound well to many Americans. He had writhed for years at the constant criticism and mockery of Texas and the South published in influential newspapers and magazines. He knew this was a handicap to his possible presidential hopes that some of the other aspirants could exploit effectively against him.

By the time he went back to the LBJ Ranch for a rest at Eastertime, Senator Johnson had been given the reports from his friends who, without formal announcement that he was a bonafide candidate, had been scouting the political centers of the country on his behalf. Their summaries showed that if his name were to be presented to the national convention, he could count on a nucleus of 319 votes from the Southern bloc, including Texas; that he seemed likely to receive perhaps 110 votes from delegates representing the border states of Maryland, Kentucky, and others, and should pick up as many as 100 other votes in places such as New Mexico, Montana, Arizona, and the Middle West in a scattered pattern. If these calculations were valid, he'd have 500 to 550 votes on the first ballot. Taking the speculation one step further, it didn't appear at that point that any of the aspirants could sweep to the nomination with 761 votes on the first ballot. Then, if there were a second ballot at the convention, Lyndon Johnson could pick up delegates who might be persuaded to switch. Or so the reasoning went.

Still, there was the chance of a bitter brawl that would leave the Democratic Party easy prey to a Richard Nixon who was waiting to become Mr. Eisenhower's Republican successor. There were uncertainties enough so that Senator Johnson continued to withhold an open announcement that he could be persuaded to run for President.

His image to Texas Democrats showed nothing of this reluctance. The LBJ emblems and badges blossomed like Texas bluebonnets at the precinct conventions of 1960, where delegates to the county conventions, pledged to support

Lyndon Baines Johnson for President, were chosen. Among die-hard Adlai Stevenson supporters in Texas the switches to Lyndon Johnson began to come thick and fast.

As one of them put it, "If I have to choose between a shrinking violet like Stevenson and a 16-cylinder Going Jesse like Lyndon Johnson, I'll take Johnson."

Almost without effort, Johnson was renominated for his Senate seat in the May primary, but the point of interest was LBJ for President.

By the time the state Democratic convention met in Austin in June, the sentiment for Johnson among almost all factions of the party was impregnable. Threats by a few anti-Johnson ultra-liberals to bolt the convention never materialized. The Texans mobilized a delegation representing all elements of Democrats and told them to prepare to go to Los Angeles and nominate their own Lyndon Johnson. "All the way with LBJ" drowned out every other problem or old feud that sunny June day at Austin.

But Senator Johnson, still cagey and still operating the Senate through a session that was stuck in presidential-election-year flypaper, continued to watch and wait.

The star of young Senator Kennedy burned brighter every day. His victories in the West Virginia and Wisconsin presidential preference primaries sparked his hard-riding organization to new levels of pressure on political figures in other states. Everywhere Johnson's outriders went to cajole delegate promises, they found a Kennedy squad had already picked up the local pledges or was coming in a few days to make the pitch for the handsome young New Englander. Either way, the Johnson men found their own efforts largely canceled out.

At last, in a feat of parliamentary magic that startled the close observers in Washington, Johnson and Speaker Rayburn recessed Congress for the month of July. This maneuver meant that instead of adjourning, or recessing until after the November election, Congress would be back in business after the presidential nominations were completed, and the winners and losers would still have to deal with Lyndon Johnson and Sam Rayburn on all legislative matters important to the fall presidential campaign. As soon as the recess began, Lyndon Johnson called a press conference to announce formally that he was a candidate for the Democratic nomination for President.

Johnson told the reporters massed in the New Senate Office Building auditorium that he had waited until this late stage to announce his candidacy because he had "a post of duty and responsibility here in Washington as the majority leader of the United States Senate, selected unanimously by all of my Democratic colleagues. Because of that duty, a duty to all the people, I cannot be absent when there is public business at stake. Those who have engaged in active campaigns since January have missed hundreds of votes [as Senators]. This I could not do. . . . Some one has to tend the store. . . ."

The Senator also said he did not intend, if nominated, to "chew on" President Eisenhower "just as I have not and I will not spend my time now trying to destroy any in my party or in other parties who might come to this high office. Mistakes have been made—and inexcusable ones. But my interest—and I believe the interest of most of my fellow Americans—is in curing those mistakes, in avoiding those mistakes, not in exploiting them for political partisan gains. . . ."

Then he prepared for the trip to Los Angeles.

The Texas phalanx for Johnson, 182 strong, headed for California and an outcome that none of them could have imagined. Mr. Rayburn, Governor Daniel and John B. Connally set up the operating headquarters at the Biltmore Hotel. This was the nerve center of the convention. Senator Kennedy and his forces held the eighth floor, Senator Johnson's suite was on the seventh floor, and the rest of the building jumped with political comings and goings starting a week before time to choose a nominee.

On his flight westward, Lyndon Johnson stopped for public interviews at the airports in Chicago and San Francisco. To the Chicago reporters he ridiculed Robert Kennedy's published prediction that the outcome of the nomination contest would be decided before the convention even opened. "This will come as a great surprise to the delegates," Johnson said. "Most of them thought they were going to Los Angeles to confer with their fellow Democrats to help select the next President."

To San Francisco reporters, Senator Johnson scoffed that the Kennedy claims of sure delegate strength had been reduced by his young rival's own statements in the last three weeks. Whereas Kennedy's men had been boasting that they had 710 convention votes assured, now they were saying the figure was 600.

But the Johnson camp never counted more than 550 votes as being lined up behind their candidate, more than 200 short of victory. When Johnson joined his fellow Texans, he took over the scurrying search for more delegates. He gave daily pep talks to the Texas crowd, issued a constant stream of instructions for them to buttonhole this politician or that. All the way through, he preached the theme that the convention should pick the best man for the job, not the one most ballyhooed.

"The next President is not going to be a talking President —or a traveling President," Johnson said whenever he could speak to groups of delegates in Los Angeles during those last frantic days. "He is going to be, and should be, a working President. His job is to convince the world—both our enemies and our allies—that America is strong and freedom is strong. He can't wring his hands that America is second-rate— because this generation is not a generation of decay. . . ."

Johnson and John Connally conceived a stratagem they thought might offset the Kennedy bandwagon rush that plainly was enveloping the Democrats at Los Angeles. They invited Senator Kennedy to meet Senator Johnson in a debate before a joint meeting of the delegates from Massachusetts and Texas, and before the television cameras. Senator Kennedy came to the ballroom, but not many of his Massachusetts group accompanied him. The confrontation of the two most prominent candidates for the nomination was almost an anti-climax.

Mr. Kennedy spoke first, expressing the hope that his race against the Republicans would find favor in Texas. This bland assumption of victory before his chief opponent seemed to jolt the Texans. Senator Johnson rejoined with a series of sarcastic jibes at Senator Kennedy's youth, inexperience, and absences from the Senate during that year. But the expected debate never materialized and the Kennedy victory psychology continued to pick up momentum among those who would be selecting a presidential nominee the following day.

The Texans, especially the conservatives among them, that same evening received another jarring lesson in who was running the 1960 convention when Chester Bowles, Senator Kennedy's foreign policy adviser, presented the party platform for adoption by the convention. The planks in that platform included strong racial integration pledges, a call for closing the door on favorable tax treatment of the oil industry, and a promise to lift "unfair" restrictions on organized labor. The flavor of labor-liberalism in the document caused deep qualms among some of the Texas delegation as they tried to imagine supporting it among the voters back home. But they still had hopes for the Johnson candidacy at that point.

The final blow fell Wednesday evening in the Los Angeles Coliseum. The nation watched by television as the roll call of the state delegations proceeded. Most of Lyndon Johnson's votes came from the Southern delegates. At 10:45 P.M. the call reached Texas. Governor Daniel announced, "Texas proudly casts sixty-one votes for Senator Lyndon B. Johnson." Five minutes later, Wyoming's votes for Senator Kennedy pushed his total past the winning mark of 761 and bedlam broke out. Few of the Texas delegates joined in the parading around the huge hall. Mr. Rayburn wiped tears from his eyes. Governor Daniel stood ramrod stiff, his fists clenched. Others expressed anger or dismay. Back in the Biltmore suite where they watched the proceedings on the television set, Lyndon and Lady Bird Johnson sat in disappointment.

Next morning at 8:30, the telephone rang in the Johnson suite. Mrs. Johnson roused from sleep and answered it. The voice was John F. Kennedy's. Might he speak to Senator Johnson? Lady Bird woke her husband. Senator Kennedy said he would like to visit the Texan. They bantered back and forth about which one would visit the other. Mr. Kennedy said he'd be right down. He came.

The new nominee asked Lyndon Johnson if he would accept the vice-presidential nomination. Johnson suggested that they both talk to their closest advisers and then come to a mutual decision. Each man realized that, in the aftermath of their final struggle for the nomination, there were persons in each camp who would recoil at the idea of the two men appearing as the party's team. Feelings had run deep and bitter in those frantic few days at Los Angeles.

Mr. Johnson conferred with Speaker Rayburn, Governor Daniel, John Connally, and a number of others. Mr. Kennedy talked to his winning team, to the party wheelhorses from the big cities. He convinced Speaker Rayburn that Johnson's presence on the ticket was essential to victory. That afternoon, the answer from both sides was "Yes."

Late in the afternoon Mr. Kennedy made the public announcement that Senator Johnson had accepted the invitation to be nominated for Vice President.

The startling responses of some delegations to Lyndon Johnson's nomination will be remembered for a long time by many persons—those who opposed him for any office, such as certain delegates from Northern and Eastern areas; most of the Texas delegation; many television viewers who saw the expressions on various faces in the convention hall. But most of the delegations whooped for joy and the celebration at the coliseum rose to a crescendo.

To most of the men who really count for something in the

machinery of the Democratic Party—David Lawrence, then governor of Pennsylvania; Mayor Richard Daly of Chicago; Mayor Robert Wagner of New York City; others of that rank —the choice of Lyndon Johnson for Vice President was exactly what they already had agreed in private meetings should happen. "On the Saturday before," Mr. Lawrence said later, "we were together [meaning the top movers and shakers of the convention] and talked it over." They all knew at that time, he said, that Senator Kennedy had won the presidential contest hands down. Their discussion sorted out the potential running mates. "Some said Lyndon Johnson wasn't liberal enough. I said, 'Look at his record. Of course he is liberal enough."

The nomination of Johnson, however, caught most experts off base, and flabbergasted most of Texas. Johnson's supporters couldn't imagine his accepting second place in anything, least of all in the presidential contest. After the first shock, however, Johnson's friends began to find the reasons to justify his running for Vice President. They told each other that, if elected, he still would have great influence in Congress. They spread the word that he would be sitting in the National Security Council alongside Mr. Kennedy and thus be at the nerve center of the nation. They said the vice presidency had been elevated to a place of world importance so that Lyndon Johnson, if elected, would hold status to which his vision and experience entitled him.

Johnson and the Democratic leaders in Texas held on to these arguments during the stormy and bitter presidential campaign of 1960. Texas played a major part in the final close result and Lyndon Johnson led in making Texas' role count in the Kennedy-Johnson victory.

Mr. and Mrs. Johnson flew to Acapulco for a brief rest after the strain of Los Angeles. Then with the energy that has made them famous, they went to work on the campaign. Mr. Johnson chartered a plane and flew thirty-seven Texas newspaper writers and publishers to Hyannis Port, Massachusetts, to visit with John F. Kennedy. He judged correctly that Kennedy's charm would have its effect on the way these news people presented the story of the autumn contest.

Talking to that group, Mr. Kennedy said that Lyndon Johnson would carry out the obligations of the vice presidency "better in the public interest than any Vice President in recent times." Johnson returned the praise in full measure.

The next Johnson campaign effort took him to an outdoors farm meeting in Iowa where he excoriated Republican farm policies, to the delight of the crowd. Mr. and Mrs.

Johnson then flew to Nashville, Tennessee, for an eight-state Democratic rally, another scene of enthusiasm. It was a swift start on the search for votes that would go on at the same hectic pace for another hundred days.

Before Senator Johnson returned to Washington to help wind up the recessed business of Congress, his neighbors in Blanco County laid on a barbecue for five thousand hill-country Texans to wish him well in the election. The governor of Texas and Congressman Homer Thornberry presented the Johnsons to the crowd after Mayor Wayne Smith of Blanco started the proceedings by calling the new Democratic slate "a kangaroo ticket, with all its strength in the hind legs." Johnson's neighbors laughed appreciatively. When Lyndon Johnson addressed the crowd, he praised John Kennedy as a "well-informed, courageous, able and diligent man . . . I have looked into his eyes more than any of you. I can tell you this: no human being in the world is going to dictate what he does. . . ." The core of Johnson's speech was a strong plea that prosperous America help feed and clothe the hungry poor of the world.

Gesturing toward the numerous small children in the crowd, Johnson said, "The children in these uncommitted countries are a lot the same as yours. The only difference is they have tapeworm and leprosy and eczema, and their daddies make only about two hundred dollars a year. . . ." This was, and still is, Lyndon Johnson's favorite theme, privately and publicly.

Johnson discussed before his neighbors the reason he accepted the vice-presidential nomination: "I didn't run for Vice President, but I have never run from anything in my life." He said it was a fair convention, he finished second, and he felt in his heart his decision was in the best interests of the nation.

"I could have taken my baseball bat and gone home, but I decided not to. . . . It's not easy to try for first place and get second . . . I thought it took a bigger man to do it than to walk out and say no. . . ."

The session of Congress produced nothing but political stalemate and the minimum necessary routine business, and then the political battle began in full array between Kennedy-Johnson and Richard Nixon-Henry Cabot Lodge. Nowhere was it more fiercely contested than in Texas, but while Lyndon Johnson labored hard and often in his own state, he also found time to fly to other parts of the nation to compaign for the Democratic cause.

While Senator Johnson flew to his many and far-flung speaking engagements, Mrs. Johnson took on a separate and full-scale assignment. Sometimes alone, sometimes with sisters of Mr. Kennedy, she visited cities in various states, talking to women's tea and luncheon gatherings about the reasons for electing Kennedy and Johnson. The campaigning marked Mrs. Johnson's emergence as a poised and charming public speaker.

The LBJ Ranch became the Johnson headquarters. Its landing strip and the highways leading to the banks of the Pedernales gave easy, ready access to the people who came for instructions and pep talks. Johnson used airplanes to come and go, added extra telephone facilities to make the big white ranch house function more efficiently as a political nerve center.

Lyndon Johnson escorted John Kennedy through Texas in mid-September on a triumphal tour. When they reached Houston, Kennedy arranged to meet a group of Protestant ministers and clarify for them his views on the separation of Church and State. This had become a burning issue in Texas where many militant Protestants held a deep fear of what might happen if a Roman Catholic were elected President of the United States. So ably did Mr. Kennedy present his conviction that Church and State should be separate in every way that he reduced the issue's dimensions, though it was a flame that continued to be fanned by numerous Texans. The film record of Mr. Kennedy's exchange with the Houston ministerial group was shown in many parts of the nation for the rest of the campaign.

The other chief opposition force in Texas took the form of "Democrats for Nixon" headed by former Governor Allan Shivers and a long list of prominent business and professional leaders, most of whom had been active in 1952 and 1956 when Mr. Eisenhower carried the state. This group centered fire on two targets, the Democratic platform, which it branded "socialism," and Lyndon B. Johnson, whom it branded a turncoat and opportunist for consenting to run on the same ticket with the liberal John F. Kennedy.

A curious fact of the campaign was that Americans for Democratic Action denounced Lyndon Johnson as a reactionary at the same time many Texans were calling him a "Northern Socialist."

These attacks only spurred Johnson to redouble his campaign efforts. On one quick swing through the Middle West, he visited former President Harry Truman in Missouri to swap ideas for increasing the campaign tempo. Mr. Truman reminded Johnson of the famously successful Truman whistle-stop railroad campaign tours of 1948. There was nothing better, he said, for dramatizing a candidate and getting into small towns where they never saw a major candidate before. Johnson decided to "whistle stop" through the South.

On a special train loaded with reporters, cameramen, political aides and all the paraphernalia for ballyhoo, Lyndon Johnson set out from Washington to campaign for the votes of the Southern states. It was a razzle-dazzle performance of a week through Virginia, the Carolinas, Georgia, Alabama, Mississippi, culminating in a huge rally at New Orleans. The headlines and broadcasts that followed the Johnson special train were an extra dividend. What really counted, besides Johnson's speeches to the Southerners, were his visits along the way with the state and local political leaders on the theme that, for their own good and the good of their people, they'd better stay with the Democratic ticket. It was language they understood without an interpreter. Johnson's forthright, vigorous salesmanship, complete with lapel-pulling, back-patting, close-up exhortation, was never in better form.

So the struggle went on. Nixon and Lodge visited Texas, and Senator Barry Goldwater made a swing through the state deriding Lyndon Johnson for seeking the vice presidency and re-election to the United States Senate at the same time. This criticism of Johnson was added to the "socialist" and "turncoat" charges as the cauldron of public sentiment bubbled higher with the approach of the November election. Johnson's speeches continued to emphasize the argument that the Democratic Party had room enough for all shades of opinion, that the party held the nation's best hope of making a better life for more Americans and more of humanity elsewhere.

In the last week of campaigning, after having appeared in forty-three states at every sort of political rally and parade, indoors and out, Lyndon Johnson spent his time touching up the Democratic cohorts in Texas.

The Senator and Mrs. Johnson drove from Fort Worth to Dallas on the morning of November 4 to address a Democratic luncheon at a downtown hotel. As their motorcade neared the principal street intersection in the heart of Dallas, they saw milling in front of the hotel a crowd of about two thousand men and women. Their first thought was that the local Democrats had turned out a good reception for them. As they reached the crowd, however, the Johnsons saw it was not a friendly gathering. Signs carried by the apparent leaders advertised "Nixon-Lodge." The Johnsons saw Republican Congressman Bruce Alger waving a sign bearing a picture of Johnson with carpetbag in hand and an inscription: "He sold out to the Yankees." The crowd made it difficult for the Johnsons to get out of their automobile, and squeezed against them on the sidewalk. There were insults and jostling. The Johnsons pushed on into the lobby of a hotel across the street from their scheduled meeting place.

Finally, Lyndon and Mrs. Johnson essayed the crossing to their luncheon engagement. Again the crowd greeted them with catcalls and insults. Some spat at them. The Johnsons went through the ordeal with forced smiles, and finally reached the safety of the Democratic meeting.

As the incident was pieced together afterward by newspaper reporters, a Republican crowd had met at Fort Worth to greet Richard Nixon at the airport. The partisans were instructed there to reassemble at the corner of Commerce and Akard Streets in downtown Dallas to heckle Senator Johnson when he arrived. Newspapers and television gave the episode extensive coverage that evening and the next morning.

The cries of outrage from Democrats all over Texas added a significant note to the final stages of the voter appeals. Mr. and Mrs. Johnson and their daughters appeared with Mr. and Mrs. Kennedy, Mrs. Franklin D. Roosevelt and others in New York City for the Democratic campaign's last touch. Then the Johnsons flew home to the LBJ Ranch to await results.

A measure of the Texas sentiment for Lyndon Johnson came in the fact that he received 1,306,625 votes for re-election to the United States Senate while the Kennedy-Johnson ticket got only 1,167,932 votes. The Nixon-Lodge vote in Texas totaled 1,121,699. After the narrow Kennedy-Johnson victory had been settled with the final count of the ballots extending for days, the two victors met in Florida to start the process of setting up a new administration. Following that, Mr. Kennedy accepted the Johnsons' invitation to fly to Texas and spend a night at the LBJ Ranch. As he stepped from the light plane that carried him from Austin to the ranch, Mr. Kennedy found a swarm of Johnson neighbors and visiting reporters pushing forward to greet him ahead of Senator and Mrs. Johnson. The mayor of the nearby hamlet of Stonewall made a quick speech of welcome and took a cowboy hat from its wrappings to present to Kennedy. The President-elect accepted the hat but laughed off the request of photographers that he put it on. He carried it in his hand as he made his way to the car that would carry him the fifty yards to the ranch house.

Next morning, Lyndon Johnson took John Kennedy deer-hunting in the brushy hills near the ranch. They returned from the hunt with deer, one of which Johnson said had been felled by Kennedy at a distance of 400 yards. The phenomenal marksmanship added color to the friendly newspaper stories about the young President-elect on his first visit to the Johnson ranch, and is still a subject for argument among deer-hunters.

The only significance to this hunting story is that it was an illustration everybody could understand of Lyndon Johnson's continued effort, in every possible way, to build up the reputation of the young man he had come to admire and under whom he was determined to do his best.

"I am going to try to be the kind of Vice President that I would want if I were President," Lyndon Johnson said. It was the guideline he followed religiously.

CHAPTER XI

Lyndon Johnson discovered at the start of his vice-presidential term that President John F. Kennedy intended to use the Johnson talents and energy in numerous assignments. The full extent of this association is known only to Johnson now, but the evidences of it were apparent from the time they were elected.

The two men kept close counsel as Mr. Kennedy chose his administration. After the inaugural week in Washington, the business of the new regime became pressing on many fronts at once. Vice President Johnson received daily summons and assignments from the President. So often was his presence required at the White House that Mr. Johnson was given a suite in the Executive Office Building next door so that he need not always travel the length of Pennsylvania Avenue when the President wanted him.

Prudently, Johnson hung on to his big Capitol office and his new Senate Office Building suite, since space was at a premium and he had besides his duty to preside over the United States Senate the charges of presiding over the National Aeronautics and Space Council and directing the work of the Committee on Equal Employment Opportunity. While the size of the staffs immediately under his direction diminished somewhat when he left the Majority Leadership, he kept the key men and women in their accustomed places and worked them as hard and long as ever on the many responsibilities given him as Vice President.

Mr. and Mrs. Johnson realized their official requirements for hospitality far exceeded the capacity of their longtime residence on 30th Place, N.W., in Washington. They purchased from Mrs. Perle Mesta her Norman house, The Elms, in the fashionable Washington residential section called Spring Valley. They spent lavishly out of their own pockets during the next three years to entertain groups of visitors ranging from rural women's leaders to the captains of industry and finance as opportunity afforded. They also took full part in Washington society's seasonal dinners and dances. Lyndon and Lady Bird Johnson like people, like to entertain and be entertained.

Lyndon Johnson's growth as Vice President and his reaction to the new experiences and influences were as marked as had been his growth as a young Senator a dozen years earlier. The inquisitive intelligence that has led him up the incline of leadership found many avenues to pursue, and Mr. Kennedy, with what seems now almost like prescience, opened the avenues best calculated to complete Lyndon Johnson's background for the presidency.

Johnson's duties in helping to shape the new and controversial space program fitted his managerial skill. The task of coordinating the needs and demands of military scientists, non-military scientists, aerospace companies—all exploring unknown regions—came under Johnson's jurisdiction. He was able, say his associates on the National Aeronautics and Space Council, to bring order out of confusion, by persuasion, by exerting his capacity for decision, by insisting on facts and on top performance.

The work of the Vice President as head of the Committee on Equal Employment Opportunity brought out his persuasiveness—firm persuasiveness—in bringing results where results had been lacking.

On the telephone and sometimes in person, from the beginning of this assignment, Johnson convinced major employers in industry to break down their historic color line and hire qualified Negroes in jobs which never before had been open to them. Johnson's belief in negotiation and person-to-person persuasion as a means of winning employment opportunities and other gains for Negroes had been evident for years. As Senator, he had proposed a federal conciliation and negotiation procedure as part of a civil rights program. Now he had a chance to prove that it could be effective. Even then, when trouble really threatened in 1963, Lyndon Johnson had an important part in dissuading the organizers of the March on Washington from staging the demonstration at the Capitol building, and in convincing them that the Lincoln Memorial was the ideal focal point.

Johnson has never had any racial prejudice in his private views. As a Senator, his record on securing voting rights for all Americans is well-known. But as Vice President, he felt the obligation to speak out, with the full consent of President Kennedy, and this Johnson did with increasing impact during 1963.

It was in his role as Chairman of the Committee on Equal Employment Opportunity that Lyndon Johnson, on Memorial Day, 1963, made one of his greatest speeches as Vice President. He addressed a crowd at Gettysburg, Pennsylvania, where a hundred years before Abraham Lincoln delivered his immortal words. Johnson's speech had its own poignant appeal for justice for all. It ended:

". . . Until justice is blind to color, until education is unaware of race, until opportunity is unconcerned with the color of men's skins, emancipation will be a proclamation but not a fact. To the extent that the proclamation of emancipation is not fulfilled in fact, to that extent we shall have fallen short of assuring freedom to the free."

Lyndon Johnson continued to speak out for equal rights and equal opportunity, before audiences in all parts of the nation during 1963. He said the same things in North Carolina and Florida that he said in Detroit and California—equal opportunities and equal treatment are the rights of every American citizen. One of his proudest moments came one day in the fall of 1963 when Mr. Kennedy asked Johnson for copies of some of his recent speeches on civil rights. "He said he wanted to borrow some of the language," Johnson said.

The Vice President, always insistent on facts whenever they can be had, brought one White House gathering down to earth in June of 1963. The subject was equal employment policies in hiring union labor. The guests included most of the leading labor union officials of the land. Johnson had drawn on his staff ahead of time for the statistics bearing on the discussion. When it came his turn to talk, he displayed the figures, showing that local unions in the construction trades in the cities of the South had more Negro members by a startling margin than did similar locals in the North and East. He suavely suggested that the thing for labor union leaders to do was to practice what they were preaching.

But it was in the field of international relations that Mr. Kennedy found a new and multi-sided role for Lyndon Johnson. One of the sides was to be a watchful and fatherly overseer of the Peace Corps, the Kennedy idea that attracted more favorable reaction than anything else he proposed. Lyndon Johnson's assignment was to help guide the necessary legislation through Congress and to help Sargent Shriver find talent to start the Peace Corps, then to assist its development.

About the time this activity began, Lyndon Johnson was asked to represent the United States in Senegal at the celebration of that African country's independence. The flying trip was a fast one but his impressions of the poverty and misery in the places he visited in Senegal are still vivid. He came home with new determination to promote, through the Peace Corps and any other possible channel, every idea that offered help to the earth's poor and backward to improve themselves. His later travels reinforced this resolve. It is a subject Johnson brings into nearly every discussion. In Senegal, as in other faraway places later, he walked among the people, in the market places, visiting their homes, shaking hands and giving away LBJ souvenir ballpoint pens. He "pressed the flesh and looked them in the eye," in his own words. Whatever memory of him they may retain, it cannot be as sharp as his own memories of their needs.

In the spring of 1961, Mr. Kennedy gave Lyndon Johnson his most difficult overseas assignment. It was a trip of negotiation and sounding-out in the countries of Southeast Asia. The fate of South Vietnam was the prime interest, but over the whole picture hung the threat of a Communist advance reaching into Southeast Asia. Mr. Kennedy entrusted to Johnson the mission of going out and reporting back.

Consequently, Vice President and Mrs. Johnson, together with diplomatic and military advisers, set off in April for their first round-the-world trip. They traveled in a jet airplane, and were trailed by another jet carrying news-media representatives. To Hong Kong and the Philippines, to Formosa, and then to South Vietnam the Vice President went, negotiating economic and military agreements at each place. His appraisal and later report on South Vietnam, particularly, turned out to be a vital prelude to the massive American intervention there against the pressing Communist offensive.

On to Thailand went the Vice President and his entourage, and then to India. At each of the stops, naturally, lavish entertainment greeted the visitors from the United States. New to the Orient, but sensing that these people were not really different from the folks back home, Lyndon Johnson took every opportunity, whenever there was a gathering, in whatever country, to see or to hail the big American and his party, to walk into the crowd, shake hands, smile and express his pleasure at being among the people. This unorthodox behavior shocked his State Department and military escorts but it pleased the people. Never before had any of them seen a high official of any kind, much less one from the faraway United States, walk among them in eager and smiling friendship. They loved it, and the news traveled.

When the Vice President and his party landed at the airport outside Karachi, Pakistan, the crowds turned out along the route to see this new kind of American. En route from the airport to the presidential palace, normally a trip of a few minutes, the Lyndon Johnson limousines quickly became entangled in a massive swarm of Pakistanis. At the first crowd-caused stop, Johnson leaped from his car and began shaking hands, pushing forward on foot with a warm smile and a constantly repeated, "Howdy . . . hi there . . . glad to see you . . . nice to meet you . . . come to see us sometime. . . ." This unfamiliar but heartwarming Texas tactic stirred even more smiles and friendliness among the Pakistanis than it had done in the other cities at previous stops.

At one street intersection, as Lyndon Johnson "shook and howdy'd" his way through the throng, he saw a sturdy, smiling man, clad in the white cotton garments of a worker, standing beside a camel-drawn cart waiting for a chance to cross the avenue with his load of sacked straw. Johnson moved forward, offered his hand with a smile, greeted the camel driver. Through an interpreter, Johnson told him that it would be a pleasure to have the camel driver visit Texas sometime. Cameramen recorded the quick meeting of the two. The episode was over in a moment and the Vice President of the United States moved along. He finally reached the presidential palace where General Mohammed Ayub Khan awaited his guest.

What neither of them realized at the time was that Pakistan's most widely read newspaper columnist had overheard Johnson's chat with the camel driver. This was to emerge later as the beginning of a new and different kind of diplomacy.

Meanwhile, Johnson and Ayub Khan found each other on the same wavelength. They frankly assessed the Communist threat in Southeast Asia. As Johnson told the story later, Ayub Khan was the only national leader he met on this entire trip who did not hesitate in saying what his country would do if full-scale hostilities broke out over Laos. "This man told me," Johnson said more than once back in the United States, "that Pakistan would furnish whatever we wanted. He told me, 'I'll send a battalion, a brigade, a division or two divisions. . . . I'll lead them myself. Just tell me what you want.'"

Along with gifts, Johnson bore to Ayub Khan an official invitation to visit the United States, and they agreed on the date. When Johnson returned to Washington, he delivered the message. President Mohammed Ayub Khan and his entourage received a lavish welcome to Washington, climaxed by a candlelit dinner given by President and Mrs. Kennedy on the lawn of Mt. Vernon.

Then Lyndon Johnson flew the president of Pakistan to Texas. Members of Johnson's efficient staff had done their part according to instructions. They invited several hundred prominent Texans to come to an outdoor barbecue at the

LBJ Ranch on the banks of the Pedernales River in honor of the president of Pakistan. Lyndon and Lady Bird Johnson and the Pakistani president arrived at the ranch on a Saturday. The big barbecue was served the next afternoon. All during the morning and early afternoon, automobiles and airplanes from all parts of Texas arrived at the LBJ. The grassy river bank in front of the big white ranch house filled with Texas bankers, lawyers, publishers, editors, political chieftains, ranchers and farmers. Some traveled 500 to 600 miles, others only 150 or 200 miles to the spot in the rugged Texas hills west of Austin, the state capital.

A pine platform decked with red, white and blue bunting and flying the U. S. and Pakistan flags at the corners, gave the crowd a focal point. Eddie Arnold, the cowboy singer, whanged his electric guitar and sang ballads. Presently, from the ranch house, emerged the Johnsons and their Pakistani and Washington guests. Johnson and Ayub Khan rode in an electric cart, Johnson driving. A Mexican mariachi band led them down the lane and into the crowd, finally reaching the platform. A long table in front of the platform afforded the place for the official party's barbecue. Then the Vice President of the United States and the president of Pakistan mounted the platform to address the relaxed but intent crowd. Their words of friendship and mutual trust struck just the proper note. The Johnsons told their neighbors and other friends of the hospitality of Pakistan on their recent visit and how strong was Ayub Khan's devotion to the free world. They showered President Ayub Khan with gifts—a western saddle and bridle, a Stetson hat, a leather jacket, and other souvenirs of the Southwest. The crowd polished off a mountain of barbecue and an appropriate quantity of beverages, and cheered every speech, every gift, every introduction.

Soon after this pleasant occasion, Vice President Johnson was reading the translations of the native Asian newspapers to gauge reactions to his visits in the countries of Asia. He came across a newspaper column in a Pakistan paper recounting the Johnson chat with a camel driver whose name, it said, was Bashir Ahmed. Just imagine, said the writer in effect, the Vice President of the United States taking time to meet a plain, humble camel driver and inviting Bashir Ahmed to Texas.

"Invite him to Texas" . . . the words seemed to stand out in neon lights.

Johnson went to work through official channels to check into the character and circumstances of this all-but-unknown Bashir Ahmed in Karachi. He also used the telephone—as only Johnson can use it—to arrange fare and other expenses, and to be sure that proper escorts were alerted in Washington, Austin and elsewhere. The story of what happened has become part of the growing accumulation of Johnson folklore.

Bashir Ahmed was flown to the United States and lionized wherever he went, Johnson at his side. He saw the sights and met the leaders in Washington and in Austin, Texas. He slept in the same bed at the LBJ Ranch that his president, General Ayub Khan, had occupied not too long before. Everywhere he went, Bashir Ahmed moved and spoke with the quiet dignity and grace which attracted Johnson originally to the people in Karachi. "They are sweet people," Johnson said in recounting the start of this unusual episode in person-to-person diplomacy. "They have poise and dignity and they are lovely to their children. . . ."

Johnson and his friends saw to it that Bashir Ahmed went home well-stocked with gifts, including a new pickup truck and other durable goods. Skeptics made light of the whole sequence of events. Some critics even sent investigators tracking the camel driver to his hut in the slums of Karachi, seeking to prove that it was a faked and ill-conceived adventure. But they came away convinced, admitting that Bashir Ahmed was everything Johnson had said he was, and more, and that the trip indeed had its origin in a coincidental communication of ideas shared by two men who didn't know each other, a newspaper columnist, and the Vice President of the United States. They furthermore conceded the propaganda impact on the people of Karachi was nothing short of terrific.

Johnson's own brand of personal diplomacy in other lands on occasion has been the cause of much comment and considerable apprehension on the part of those who believe diplomacy is a matter of protocol. The following State Department report on the results of his visit early in 1963 to the Dominican Republic should be comforting to the fearful ones:

Embassy considers Vice President's visit outstanding success both from point of view of public relations and impact on new GODR (Government of Dominican Republic) reception accorded him by crowds of ordinary Dominicans and his response thereto constituted in embassy's opinion a triumph for U. S. in Dom. Rep.

Press made much of fact that Vice President embraced President Bosch in the Latin American manner . . . President Bosch was pleased and obviously impressed by gift of ambulance presented by Vice President in name of American people to Dominican Republic people . . . Mrs. Johnson's visits to school for blind and maternity hospital were thoroughly covered by television and press. . . .

Six or seven months ago would have been unlikely that Vice President of United States could drive through city without arousing demonstration of hostility. Johnson's unaffected mixing with crowds caused strong and favorable impact.

Months later, Johnson was much disquieted over the sudden coup d'etat that removed President Bosch from office. His private reaction, in the light of the later fact of his presidency, may be taken as an indication that a firmer United States policy toward overthrow of governments in this hemisphere can be expected.

In August of 1961 when the Wall created a crisis in Berlin, Mr. Kennedy asked Lyndon Johnson to fly to that city and give the people official public assurances that the United States would not abandon West Berlin. Johnson made the trip, addressed a huge crowd of Berliners in a way that did much for their morale. Mayor Willy Brandt said later that Lyndon Johnson's arrival meant much more to the people of West Berlin than the arrival of 1,500 additional United States troops about the same time.

The next major overseas assignment from the President took Lyndon Johnson to Turkey, Greece, and Italy about a year later. He bore Washington's word that in view of their improving economies, these nations, particularly Greece, should start paying more of the military expenses necessary to safeguard them from Communist attack. It was an assignment which Lyndon Johnson carried out to the letter, though he said when he returned that it wrenched him to give the bad news to the officials he visited. He came home with spoken admiration for the calm courage of the Turkish people, and of the people of Greece, whom he described as looking down the Communist gun barrel every morning before breakfast.

And a scene in Italy became a part of Johnson's conversational report on his journey. As he described it, a group of nuns led a huge crowd of children to see his motorcade near Naples. "They stopped our cars," he said. "They didn't know me from Adam but they wanted to thank the American for what the United States had done to restore their families and homes after the war."

Correspondence between Lyndon Johnson and John Kennedy dealing with the young President's assignments of "overseas chores", as he phrased it, is revealing of the mutual respect they held for each other.

After his visits in Southeast Asia, India and Pakistan, Johnson wrote a detailed analytical resume of the position of the United States in those troubled areas. It foretold, in 1961, much of the deterioration that has occurred since, and counseled the firmest steps to prevent American influence from being forced back across the Pacific.

The Vice President wrote similar memoranda after his later missions made in the President's behalf. Lyndon Johnson went on these fact-finding flights with power to negotiate and to act when necessary.

Mr. Kennedy's replies to the Johnson reports were warmly commendatory. He said the Vice President "was a prisoner of his own success" and would be called upon to continue such overseas missions.

Johnson by that time was telling everybody he talked to, in speeches, and in private chats, that wherever he went in other countries he found friendliness and admiration for the United States. "We are the best-loved people on earth. We ought to appreciate it and do something about it," he said frequently.

Johnson's optimism that the poor of the earth can be helped materially is based on his own experience. He never hesitates to point out that his native Texas hill country was, in modern context, undeveloped and backward. More than half the land in the county was mortgaged. There were no such things as electricity or decent roads, and hardly any cash money.

"It takes the kind of faith Franklin D. Roosevelt had in us," he will tell his audience. "I went to Mr. Roosevelt one time when I was a young Congressman and asked him to include in his budget a million dollars for a dam down on the Pedernales River. He had his experts look into it and they said it wasn't in the pattern, that there had to be a 'density' of three people to the square mile in order to qualify for the dam. Mr. Roosevelt told them to go ahead with the money, that the folks down in those hills would breed pretty fast. . . ."

The technical revolution that transformed the Southwest can transform other parts of the world, Lyndon Johnson believes. One of his pet dreams is the de-salting of sea water. He put the main impetus behind the experimental government program in that field. The first de-salting plant was built on the Gulf coast of Texas. Johnson flew down from

Washington to dedicate the plant and make a speech on the blessings of science.

Nor did his active interest in all these things keep Lyndon Johnson from presiding over the United States Senate when key issues came before it.

A typical Johnson performance came early in 1963 as the Senate went through its annual battle over the filibuster. Johnson had been through this intricate struggle numerous times before as the Democratic Party leader in the Senate, had saved the freedom of debate in that august body, once by a brilliant compromise that gave the losers a crumb of comfort. But now he would be obligated to wield the limited power of the Vice President as the presiding officer of the Senate so as to reflect credit on his party and himself and do no harm to the Senate or the nation. This is a more difficult assignment than anybody but an expert in the Senate rules and traditions can appreciate.

Johnson, the master of the Senate during his days as Democratic leader, knew better than anybody else the pitfalls that awaited him as the outnumbered and already beaten liberal Senators prepared to try before the public, their case for limiting debate in the Senate.

Johnson called for advice in writing from parliamentarians, Senate experts, constitutional authorities and others. He took the pile of papers home with him, then to Camp David in the Maryland hills.

Far into the night, and again before daylight, Johnson studied the mass of suggestions and warnings and recitations of precedent and constitutional law. His elephantine memory, with its background of Senate wisdom, soaked up every nuance of every possibility that could confront him in the crucial final week of the rules battle. His rulings would not encroach on the jealously guarded rights of the Senators. They would not be blatantly partisan, yet they would not help the opposition. And that is the way it turned out. When the liberals had gone down to inevitable defeat, they turned on Johnson in a flurry of angry speeches, accusing him of improper conduct in their last effort to unload frustration and find a scapegoat. Thanks to Johnson's careful preparations and his meticulous handling of the chairman's role, his defenders in the Senate could, and did, throw back at his critics the chapter and verse of his correct performance.

Writing of Johnson's research in depth in preparing for this challenge, Jim Mathis of the Newark, New Jersey, *Star-Ledger,* commented:

The fact that Lyndon Baines Johnson, Vice President, labored there in the guarded loneliness of a seldom-used Presidential residence in the early hours of a January morning upon his only constitutionally assigned task, illustrates two unappreciated features of the man and the office:

1. Johnson, at 54, is energetic and as competitive as ever, will labor mightily to master any task given him.

2. The greatly expanded scope and responsibility of the Vice Presidency under President Kennedy leave little time for presiding. . . .

Lyndon Johnson came back from his 1961 round-the-world trip to learn that in a sequence of freakish political circumstances, Texas had elected a Republican to the United States Senate. It was a traumatic experience for the state's acknowledged Democratic kingpin to contemplate that his prized Senate seat now belonged to a Republican. Whatever his feelings, however, he concealed them in perfect decorum when it fell his lot to preside over the Senate ceremony in which young John Tower of Witchita Falls took the oath of office.

The denouement resulted in Lyndon Johnson's keeping a closer eye on local Texas politics than he ever had done before, and this is saying volumes about close scrutiny. Johnson knew without asking that the Republican sentiment in Texas had received its greatest stimulus from John Tower's election. Johnson had no political machine, because Texas politics doesn't work in that manner. But he had friends and sources of information, and he resolved that he would do what he could in the future to assist Democrats when they faced Republican opposition.

This assistance to Texas Democrats from the Vice President of the United States took whatever form seemed appropriate at the time. In one contest, when Graham Purcell was the Democratic candidate for a seat in Congress from Witchita Falls, Lyndon Johnson decided the only requirement was that Judge Purcell receive a diagram of how to win his runoff election campaign against a Republican opponent. Johnson invited the tall, quiet-spoken judge to the LBJ Ranch. After Mrs. Johnson had served the coffee, Lyndon Johnson began his instructions. He covered every aspect of a campaign, from the proper way to shake hands to the details of staging political rallies and preparing advertising in all media and persuading friends to join the campaign.

The meeting gave Graham Purcell a master's degree in

politics, which he proceeded to validate by winning his election to Congress.

A more spectacular example of the way Lyndon Johnson came to the aid of Democratic candidates for Congress in Texas unfolded in San Antonio after the veteran Congressman Paul Kilday resigned to accept a military claims court appointment. The unexpired term attracted State Senator Henry Gonzalez as the Democratic candidate and a young San Antonio businessman as the Republican candidate.

San Antonio's large Latin population seemed no guarantee for Gonzalez' victory. The Republican organization there was well-trained, well-financed and energetic. Lyndon Johnson got busy. He gathered and delivered campaign funds to Gonzalez' organization. He brought in the international movie star, Cantinflas, from Mexico to attract crowds on behalf of Gonzalez. And Lyndon Johnson took the stump himself, for a whole day and evening, making speeches on street corners in various parts of the city for Gonzalez with the candidate by his side.

The climaxing speech and its aftermath gave Johnson one of his favorite anecdotes:

In their final appearance that evening, Johnson and Gonzalez harangued the listeners from the bed of a pickup truck parked at an intersection in a Negro residential area. When they had done their best, Johnson thought the meeting was ended.

Suddenly an elderly Negro climbed into the bed of the truck. He raised both hands for silence. Tears streamed down his face.

"I was born just a few doors from this corner," the old Negro began. "I have lived for nearly sixty years right here in this neighborhood. I have seen many things, many wonderful things happen. But never in my wildest dreams did I ever imagine the time when the Vice President of the United States would stand on this street corner and ask a crowd of Negroes to elect a man named Gonzalez to any office. I can die happy now. I have seen it all."

Gonzalez won the seat in Congress and was re-elected the next year to a full term.

Johnson not only helped elect Congressmen from Texas as and when he could for the good of the Democratic Party; he assigned his veteran staff in Washington to help them organize their offices and learn how to keep in fruitful contact with their constituents. Nobody could have done this more effectively.

Mr. Kennedy's own talented associates, by the way, impressed Lyndon Johnson from the time he first saw them in action at the Los Angeles convention. He watched them bury his own presidential nomination hopes, and afterward said, "I wish I had some people like that."

During his vice presidential service, Mr. Johnson became closely acquainted with all of the Kennedy people and acquired new insights into efficiency and intelligence. In spite of the continual rumors, gossip, and other attempts to paint Mr. Johnson as being out of favor with the late President's most trusted aides, the Kennedy and Johnson teams had excellent working relationships based on mutual respect.

A deep trust and confidence grew up between Mr. Kennedy and Mr. Johnson. The Texan remained true to his pledge to "be the kind of Vice President I would want if I were President." He always responded with vigor to any Kennedy suggestion or request. Overseas errands, political speeches in any part of the nation, White House conferences on any subject—Lyndon Johnson was available to the best of his ability.

Senator Robert S. Kerr, one of Johnson's close friends in the Senate and a devout Baptist, wrote a "Prayer for My Pastor," including such lines as "Let me be a pillar of strength to help hold him up and not a thorn in his flesh to sap his strength, nor a burden on his back to pull him down. . . . Let me work for him and not compel him to spend precious time in bragging on me. . . ."

After Senator Kerr's death early in 1963, Lyndon Johnson circulated copies of the Kerr prayer, with the remark, "That's the way I feel toward my President."

Mr. Kennedy's insistence on his Vice President's being knowledgeable in every aspect of the presidency produced new respect for the office in Lyndon Johnson, who already had been close to presidents. He sometimes told friends about sitting in on discussions of critical problems. "I didn't do any talking and I am glad I wasn't called on to talk . . . that was a tough one." Or, "It makes your hair stand on end to see what responsibilities the President has to carry on his back. . . ."

But the net effect was apparent on that tragic Friday in Dallas. Stunned with grief and horror over the sudden death of his vibrant, intelligent young President, Lyndon Johnson never hesitated, never had to grope, in taking over the burdens himself.

CHAPTER XII

On the bright, cold morning of November 25, 1963, as preparations began in Washington for the funeral ceremonies to honor and bury John Fitzgerald Kennedy, President Lyndon Johnson came to his office in the Executive Office Building adjoining the White House. He had time for an hour of work before the Kennedy cortege, horsedrawn the mile from the Capitol, reached the White House, and he used the hour to the full in personal conferences and telephones calls to key figures in the government.

Outside the office, Secret Service men bustled about. No, they told those who asked, Mr. Johnson would not be allowed to walk behind the Kennedy casket with the heads of state from all over the world. He would ride in a closed sedan to the cathedral.

The caisson bearing Mr. Kennedy's coffin swung into the White House driveway, stopped for a brief time in front of the mansion, then the gray horses drew it out the other side of the drive and onto Pennsylvania Avenue.

Behind the caisson came princes and presidents; premiers, kings and queens, the leaders of the free world's nations, on foot and striding along behind the caisson.

In their midst walked President and Mrs. Johnson, side by side. Secret Service agents flanked them, looking anxiously at the rooftops and along the curbs where crowds of people stood.

This was the first public demonstration by the new President that he, not the Secret Service nor any other subordinate, would make the decisions. It was a demonstration not apparent to many. But other proofs followed swiftly in the next days and weeks showing beyond a doubt that the President was his own man, and that he knew how to reach his objectives.

Lyndon Johnson spelled out the major goals in his address to the joint session of Congress two days after Mr. Kennedy's funeral (see appendix). "Let us continue," he said, "toward the civil rights law, the tax reduction and the medical care breakthrough that Mr. Kennedy had requested of the Congress."

In a passage not fully appreciated that morning, Lyndon Johnson told the Congress that the time had come for "strong, forward-looking action on the pending foreign aid bill, making clear that we are not forfeiting our responsibilities to this Hemisphere or to the world, nor erasing executive flexibility in the conduct of foreign affairs . . ." In another month, he showed the Congress that he meant it, showed this in a way that again proved who was in the saddle.

But there were other decisions, many of them, in the meantime. One of the first steps was to make sure that the fullest possible investigation of the assassination of Mr. Kennedy, and the slaying of Lee Harvey Oswald, was made. To this end, the new President persuaded a reluctant Chief Justice Earl Warren of the United States Supreme Court to become chairman of a special presidential commission, and then persuaded other hand-picked members to serve in this onerous, time-consuming but vital search for the full story of whatever had led up to the unthinkable deeds.

There was a new national budget to be formulated, and a legislative program to be framed, and a State of the Union message to be drafted, and a constant watch to be kept upon the turbulent world outside the United States, a world strewn with powder trains that, once ignited, could blow up the planet.

Into these perplexing, difficult problems Lyndon Johnson plunged with the enormous energy and determination and capacity for absorbing knowledge in detail that had brought him to the top of the political pyramid. While he set his inherited staff and Cabinet to work on their assignments, he continued to touch all the available centers of national power himself to show as much reassurance as he could give of a continuity of purpose and strength in the presidency.

On December 4, for example, only a week after his first address to the Congress, Lyndon Johnson summoned leaders of the labor union movement and the business community to the White House for separate meetings. To the 29-man AFL-CIO Executive Council that morning, he proclaimed the objective of assisting the nation to reach a total of 75,000,000 jobs and told them that the proposed tax reduction "is the most massive single attack we can make on this problem . . ."

To 90 members of the Business Council that afternoon, the new President said: "This administration wants to help you. We are not pro-labor or pro-business, or pro-any-special-sector. We are pro-what-is-best for America . . . in employment. Let us together enlarge our economy by persuading Congress to cut taxes. . . . This nation and your President need your energy and your ingenuity. . . ."

The next day Mr. Johnson announced that he had reached

a disability agreement with House Speaker John W. McCormack on temporary succession to the presidency in the event that President Johnson were disabled. Again he was showing publicly his concern that the nation need have no fear that its principal executive office would go empty.

A few days later, Mrs. Jacqueline Kennedy and her small children moved out of the White House and the new presidential family moved in, minus older daughter Lynda who was attending the University of Texas. In the process of getting acquainted with all the details of the official residence, President Johnson discovered that the monthly White House electric bill ran to an average of $4,600 a month. This not only shocked him to his toes, this man whose childhood had known only kerosene lamplight, but it gave him a quickly-seized opportunity to dramatize his devotion to economy in the public interest. He issued orders for all White House lights to be turned off in rooms where nobody happened to be at the moment. He made such a public fuss about turning off the lights that quipsters began calling him "Lightbulb Johnson."

Almost simultaneously, President Johnson met with his Cabinet and issued orders for the strictest economies in the next budgets for the executive departments. He told them to hold their civilian employment levels below current totals and to make further savings. He took special pains to remind the Department of Defense that since it was spending half the national budget, it had a double obligation to achieve the largest savings. With Kermit Gordon, director of the budget, at his side, Mr. Johnson began the incredible task of going over every line of every page of the mammoth federal budget. He used his personal blue pencil on many proposed expenditures.

Within a few days, the White House announced that newly-motivated government officials had lopped off $750 millions in 48 hours from their intended budgetary requests for the next fiscal year. President Johnson let it be known that by January he hoped to reach a budget of not more than $102 billions or $103 billions. This would represent an increase of $4 to $5 billions over the last Kennedy budget . . . but it was only the beginning of a 30-day buildup toward a Johnson coup aimed at convincing economy-minded Congressmen that the nation could afford a tax reduction. Of that, more later.

In between all these time-consuming exercises in executive leadership, Lyndon Johnson arranged to place the family business holdings in an irrevocable trust for so long as he held federal elective office or until his death. The trustees had power to do anything they thought best with the broadcasting properties owned by Mrs. Johnson and her daughters, and to do likewise with the land and securities owned by the President.

Having got hold of the necessary levers of national and family matters through a rush of crowded days and nights of labor, Mr. Johnson turned to the world scene. On December 17, he journeyed to New York to address the United Nations General Assembly with a ringing reaffirmation of American goals: an end to the cold war, continued search for world peace, expanded nuclear weapons controls and support of the U.N. "as the best instrument yet designed to promote the peace of the world and to promote the well-being of mankind. . . ."

Five days later the official 30-day mourning period for President Kennedy ended in a twilight candle-lit ceremony at the Lincoln Memorial where the new President told the country: "We buried Abraham Lincoln and John Kennedy, but we did not bury their dreams or their visions. They are our dreams and our visions today, for President Lincoln and John Kennedy moved toward those nobler dreams where the needs of the people dwell."

Through all these days of hectic activity, the people of the United States saw a somber, dignified and busy chief executive whose appearance fitted the mood of America in the aftermath of great shock and sudden change. But a stubborn House of Representatives, refusing to go along with the new President's requested foreign aid bill and its provision for presidential authority over proposed wheat trade with the Soviet Union, stung the old whipcracking Lyndon Johnson into action.

No sooner had the House apparently turned down the presidential version of this bill than the President and his aides went to work on the members of the House . . . by telephone, by emissary, by personal confrontations; by special airplanes sent to fetch Christmas-bound Congressmen; by every known device, the President obtained another run in the House for his measure. The climax came in a 7 A.M. session of the House in which he was given what he asked. It was what he had demanded in his first speech to the Congress a month earlier, including "executive flexibility in the conduct of foreign affairs."

With this victory at his belt, President Johnson took his family to the family ranch in Texas for Christmas and a 12-day "vacation". Except for Christmas Day when relatives swarmed the ranch house (and the President took visiting reporters

111

on a tour that delayed the family dinner for two hours), the indications of a "vacation" were few and far between. Not only did the President keep a procession of White House staff members and Cabinet officers coming through the gates of the LBJ Ranch for work sessions day and night; he also had the new chancellor of West Germany fly in for two days of conferences and festivities.

For this latter event, the President himself acted as producer and director of a series of entertainments highlighted by a barbecue, piano performances by Van Cliburn and Johnson's press secretary, Pierre Salinger; folk dances and German songs by school girls from nearby Fredericksburg, all to the astonishment of most of the White House press corps who were on their first visit to the hill country of Texas.

By this time, after about six weeks in office at the most whirlwind of paces, Lyndon Johnson made it apparent to all that he was thriving under the burdens of the presidency. "I've cut my weight from 226 pounds to 203," he proudly told reporters. "I manage to get enough sleep . . . most times. I never felt better." Oldtime friends observed that he hadn't looked so well in years. Gone were the second-fiddle frustrations of the vice presidency and the uncertainties of the last years of his senatorial career. For the first time in his life, one of his old friends observed, Lyndon Johnson has enough to keep him busy and obviously it is good for him.

During his work-vacation at the ranch that Christmas season, the President divided his attention between his forthcoming messages to Congress, the new federal budget and a spate of overseas flare-ups. The situation in South Viet Nam was growing worse. Greece, Turkey and Cyprus whirled around in a blood feud that threatened to burst apart the Mediterranean end of the North Atlantic Treaty Alliance. All of this called for presidential attention and the coming and going of defense and state department leaders at the big white house on the Pedernales.

Yet the effect of being in his home country visibly buoyed up Lyndon Johnson in those busy holidays. He returned to Washington with a fresh tan and even more vigor than had been apparent, which was plenty.

Hardly had the President reached the White House when bloody anti-United States rioting broke out in Panama. American soldiers and Panamanian citizens were killed. The cool but intense treatment given this situation by President Johnson was aided especially by his new special assistant for Latin American affairs, Thomas C. Mann. By refusing to panic, by refusing to over-compensate for the accusations

112

against the United States and through a personal visit to the scene by Mann and other Johnson emissaries, this fire was put out rather quickly.

Those involved in dealing with the Panamanian crisis were impressed by a side of Lyndon Johnson that casual outsiders usually miss: his absolute passion for facts, all the facts and all the implications of the facts. Once he had them, his calm fairness to the President of Panama opened the way for a cooling-off and a subsidence of something which the Communist element on the scene had hoped to fan into a source of major embarrassment to the United States.

The Panama trouble came as President Johnson was receiving plaudits for his first State of the Union message to Congress. In it, he announced major cuts in federal spending —ahead of his budget message which was to follow—and revealed that in the process of making these reductions he had allowed enough money for "the most federal support in history for education, for health, for retraining the unemployed and for helping the economically and physically handicapped."

Lyndon Johnson in that speech told the Congress that his administration "today, here and now, declares unconditional war on poverty in America, and I urge this Congress and all Americans to join with me in that effort."

Two weeks later in his first presidential budget message, Mr. Johnson let fall his blockbuster: the new federal budget came to $97.9 billions, a figure even smaller than Mr. Kennedy's last budget; a figure that halved the annual federal deficit to $4.9 billions; a figure that, all observers agreed, assured the passage by Congress of the tax reductions which Mr. Kennedy had sought in vain during 1963.

The observers were correct. Congress required only a month to write the tax cut bill into law.

At the same time, the House of Representatives cleared the civil rights bill and sent it to the Senate, where certain filibuster awaited. But the President knew that after the filibuster had done its best, he'd have what he wanted. He won after the Senate debated the question of civil rights for 83 days and the bill for 66 days. Final vote for passage in the Senate was 73 yea, 27 nay, generally matching the margin by which the House then quickly accepted the Senate version of the civil rights measure, 289 for and 126 against. The final draft was sped to the White House that evening.

Mr. Johnson signed the civil rights bill into law on July 2, 1964. He used 72 pens to etch his signature on the measure in a televised ceremony attended by more than 200 lawmakers, civil rights leaders and government officials. To the

113

national audience and those on the scene, the President solemnly said:

"We have come now to a kind of testing. We must not fail. Let us close the springs of racial poison. Let us pray for wise and understanding hearts. Let us lay aside irrelevant differences and make our nation whole.

"Let us hasten that day when our unbounded spirit will be free to do the great works ordained for this nation by the just and wise God who is the Father of all."

He appealed for voluntary compliance with provisions of the law for equal rights and equal treatment of all American citizens, and predicted that this would be given "because most Americans are law-abiding citizens who want to do what is right."

Racial troubles lay ahead, as the President realized. But he also knew, from his careful checking with key personages in all parts of the nation, by reading the public opinion polls and by his own deep instinct for what people really believe, that the majorty of citizens were with him on civil rights. Summer primary elections in Tennessee and Georgia further bore this out when Congressmen who had voted for the civil rights bill were re-nominated over opponents who made that the main issue in the two contests.

On the congressional front, by the time the 88th Congress adjourned in October, it had given President Johnson virtually every major measure for which he had asked, with one major exception. This was the medical care bill originated by Mr. Kennedy and bottled up in a hostile committee of the House. The failure to act only reinforced Mr. Johnson's determination. As the 89th Congress moved into its agenda in 1965, high on the priority list was the medical care proposal, considerably broadened from its original terms, and the betting in Washington was that it would be law before much more time elapsed.

From January to November, 1964, Lyndon B. Johnson continued to perform at the same bewildering pace the many demanding obligations of the presidency. He learned, under Mrs. Johnson's quietly firm urging, to take a nap after lunch. He took easily to the White House swimming pool for preprandial dips and delighted to take a few friends with him to paddle around in the heated water. A warm swim, a light lunch and a sound sleep of an hour put him in shape to go headlong again until midnight. The evenings as often as not included dinner parties in the state dining room, followed by dancing in the East Room, or an occasional movie. But invariably after the guests departed, the President put in another hour or two of official reading and sometimes post-midnight telephone conversations on pressing matters.

The Johnson style of entertaining at the White House fascinated observers for its variety, its mixture of jazz and the classics in musical programming, along with a folksinging hootnanny now and then. The Johnsons paid special attention to all members of Congress, showed them all over the White House when they came for dinner or entertainment. Indeed, the first family exhibited consistent interest in opening White House hospitality to as many and as varied persons as possible.

The routine included guided tours of the family living quarters on the second floor of the mansion, with a chance to stand on "Harry Truman's balcony". "It's the prettiest view from any part of the White House," the President insists.

These upstairs excursions taught the Johnson daughters, Lynda and Luci, to wear housecoats or more at all times. After stepping out of their bedrooms and finding themselves face-to-face with a group of startled visitors in the evenings, the girls became careful indeed of their style of dress.

On tables and shelves, visitors found white folders of matches imprinted in gold: "The President's House". Thousands of the folders went into pockets and handbags as souvenirs of a memorable evening in the White House during 1964.

For state dinners, especially those honoring dignitaries from overseas, Mr. and Mrs. Johnson often invited guests from cities far removed from Washington, mostly friends of past years among the political, financial and business centers of the nation. Instead of long, formally accoutred dinner tables, they employed intimate tables for six or eight so that communication among the guests was easier and more pleasant.

Mrs. Johnson expressed the highest admiration for the manner in which Mrs. John Kennedy had decorated and re-arranged the White House. She has done little thus far to alter it but has concentrated on making its beauties and historic treasures better known and more accessible to more citizens. From the first day she moved into the mansion, Mrs. Johnson has kept a sizeable staff of secretaries and aides busy trying to help her meet the demands from citizens for appearances, speeches and other kinds of communication with the First Lady. In her own fields of endeavor and in her own quiet manner, she has worked as long and as arduously as Lyndon Johnson himself since November, 1963.

In operating the presidential office, Lyndon Johnson let his Cabinet know from the outset that he expected the department heads to assume active responsibility on their own. Likewise, he made far more use of the National Security Council than had his predecessor. But he also managed to keep a finger on all their operations, to insure that they spoke publicly in the same general vein and that the President wouldn't be caught unaware by problems large or small. To a degree seldom seen in modern government, Lyndon Johnson is his own chief of staff, his own press expert and a man of all work.

Johnson extended this all-seeing, all-knowing touch to the preparations of the Democratic National Committee for the 1964 presidential election campaign. Over a period covering most of the spring months, he amalgamated Johnson people with Kennedy people in the party's control tower so that by the time the national convention came on, his team was tuned up and ready. John Bailey, national committee chairman, and Richard Maguire, its treasurer, both Kennedy New Englanders, pulled in double harness with Cliff Carter of Texas. Kenneth O'Donnell and Walter Jenkins—again Kennedy and Johnson in harmony—operated from adjoining White House offices. The same blend was achieved across the country in naming state campaign coordinators. Information and instructions and intelligence flowed through carefully-arranged channels from the White House to the local precinct level.

Not that there wasn't occasional heartburn. Early in the year, Mr. Johnson used full pressure behind the scenes to prevent a beloved Texas Congressman—Rep. Joe Kilgore of McAllen—from coming out as a rival candidate to the much more liberal U.S. Senator Ralph Yarborough in Texas. The squeeze play infuriated conservative Texas Democrats but the realists among them, after a few weeks of fuming anger, resigned themselves to the Johnson rule.

The machinery of national politics posed no real problems to Lyndon Johnson. He had been through it before to the point where his decisions came almost automatically. Of much more concern to him was how to articulate in a meaningful way his deep sense of mission as president.

The "war on poverty" which he proclaimed in January didn't seem to him to tell adequately the way he felt. His often-repeated expression, "I want to be the president of all the people," or its variations, left something to be desired, he knew.

In mid-April, President Johnson invited the membership of the American Society of Newspaper Editors to the White House for a Friday evening of cocktails, buffet and dancing. The instructions said they were to assemble in the Rose Garden, then in gorgeous array of flowering trees, tulips and other spring blossoms. Several hundred editors and their wives gathered in the grass bordered by the flowers. The President, standing at the west side of the garden, introduced his wife and daughters, then launched into what was virtually a sermon on the theme of brotherhood and justice. The sight of middle-aged ladies standing shakily with spike heels sinking in the soft lawn, bees buzzing around their heads, didn't slow him down. In his appeal for the things he was trying to push through Congress, the President mentioned more pay for the dedicated men of government, a chance for education and jobs for the disadvantaged, and the civil rights bill. He tried out the following line for size:

"Justice is a universal beginning for a great society . . ."

A few editorials the next day mentioned this part of his speech. Most of the news coverage, however, dwelt on the gay evening that followed once he had led the assemblage indoors. It was a blast, as the younger guests expressed it. The president danced with almost every woman in the room—— the stately East Room——while a Dixieland band virtually peeled the paint off the walls.

Four days later, another group of newspaper and broadcasting executives stood in the Rose Garden, invited there from one of the periodic foreign affairs conferences held by the Department of State. On this occasion, President Johnson's address included this sentence:

"Oh, how I would like to feel that we could, here in this Rose Garden today, launch a new movement to develop a greater society in all the world."

Subsequently over the next few days before a variety of audiences, Mr. Johnson referred in one way or another to "a great society". Public reaction widened and was so favorable that the president decided to use "a great society" as the label for his domestic program and goals. He was to address an audience—it turned out to be 90,000 persons—at University of Michigan on May 22. There he made his first full-fledged "Great Society" speech.

To the Michigan listeners, President Johnson said:

"I want to talk to you today about three places where we begin to build the Great Society—in our cities, in our countryside and in our classrooms."

He went on to say that cities were suffering from decay at their cores, despoiling of suburbs, inadequate housing and inadequate transportation. Open land was vanishing and old landmarks were violated. Worst of all, he said, expansion is

117

eroding the "precious and time-honored values of community with neighbors and communion with nature."

"The loss of these values breeds loneliness and boredom and indifference," he said.

In the countryside, the President said, natural beauty is in danger of being lost; the water, food and air are threatened with pollution. Parks are overcrowded, seashores overburdened.

And in the third specified area—the classrooms—every child must be given a place to sit and a teacher to learn from, he said, adding:

"Poverty must not be a bar to learning, and learning must offer an escape from poverty."

While the intellectuals and commentators chewed on this speech with criticisms depending on their points of view, the reaction from his crowd of 90,000 at Michigan and the reaction from all the sources of information that a president can marshal convinced Lyndon Johnson that he had his themesong for 1964's election contest. Armed with that idea, and the civil rights law, and a pledge of medical care for the aged next time, he was ready to go to the country against whoever might challenge him for the 1964-68 occupancy of the White House.

The economy of the United States continued to set new and dazzling records of prosperity, the troubles overseas seemed to pose no imminent threat to the status quo and the President, of whom an aide said, "he has a great river of compassion flowing through all his veins," looked forward confidently to the verdict of the voters.

At the beginning of August, 1964, the North Vietnamese gunboat fleet removed from politics what had appeared to be a sure campaign issue for the Republican nominees. The North Vietnamese gunboats attacked U.S. Navy destroyers on patrol in the Gulf of Tonkin. The destroyers fired on them. President Johnson ordered navy forces in the area strengthened. Three days later, another gunboat attack against U.S. navy vessels in the same waters brought, on Johnson's orders, a slashing naval air attack on the gunboats' bases in North Vietnam.

Lyndon Johnson took the nation into his confidence in a national broadcast on the evening of August 4 to announce the retaliatory strikes which he had ordered in North Vietnam. All his actions in those days of tension were made carefully, if quickly, and were made public so that no misunderstanding could be charged to a lack of information. President Johnson emphasized that the retaliation policy was limited, that he sought "no wider war".

Among his preparatory moves at the height of the crisis was to get an agreement from Senator Goldwater that he endorsed Johnson's actions. Congressional approval of this "limited, fitting response" to the gunboat attacks was swift.

The interminable conflict in South Viet Nam thus moved into another phase, one which didn't reach the flash point again until after the election. Meantime, Lyndon Johnson's sure touch had give the American posture in South Viet Nam a stronger appearance.

CHAPTER XIII

Almost from the day he became President of the United States and demonstrated so swiftly his mastery of the responsibilities of office, Lyndon B. Johnson was considered a certain candidate for election in his own right. Certainly he was so considered among the Democratic Party leaders in whose hands the choice rested if they desired to make a choice. But Mr. Johnson, busy with many other concerns for the first four and a half months of his sudden term, said nothing publicly on the subject until the middle of April.

In his first televised press conference at the State Department auditorium, the President for the first time indicated that he would be a candidate for a four-year term on his own. He told the 512 reporters and editors present that he was enjoying his work and was "prepared to continue."

A few months later, a questioner referred to a poll of editors which indicated broad expectations of a Johnson victory at the polls in November and the President commented, "I hope that they feel in November as they do in April." To the limit of his ability, Lyndon Johnson continued every day to preserve and enhance his growing acceptance as President.

The following week Mr. Johnson took keen delight in announcing the end, after marathon bargaining sessions at the White House, of the four and a half-year railroad labor dispute. It had threatened to bring on a nationwide railroad shutdown by strike. As the threat verged on reality, Mr. Johnson had persuaded both sides to come to the White House and seek a settlement. For 15 days he virtually kept them locked in a room together. Occasionally he visited the bargaining sessions to exhort a settlement. Final agreement on April 22 was acclaimed across the country as Lyndon B. Johnson's most important and most dazzling personal domestic victory since he assumed the presidency.

One member of the negotiating team for the railroad workers was asked what Lyndon Johnson said in his visits to the bargaining table. "He grabbed the American flag and ran around the room," said the labor veteran. "He said we just had to keep the railroads running and the country booming."

Just before the spectacular railroad settlement, the President had announced an agreement with the Soviet Union for freezing nuclear weapon production. . .

It seemed that a day could not pass without Lyndon Johnson's furnishing the number one news story. He was playing the national and international keyboards like a steam piano. His presidential stock soared steadily while the Republicans fought bitterly among themselves for the assignment of opposing him.

Mr. Johnson kept his own counsel about the opposition party. He made· no audible predictions as to the outcome of the Republican National Convention. He had crossed swords with Richard Nixon before, on other battlefields, and had won both times—once in the senatorial elections of 1954 when they were unofficial adversaries behind other candidates and again in 1960 when, as Nixon later said publicly, Lyndon Johnson made possible the victory of John F. Kennedy. Mr. Johnson also knew Senator Barry Goldwater from their eight years in the Senate. The President regarded the Arizonan as a decent person but a rank novice in politics.

After the Republican blood-letting in San Francisco, it became even more apparent that Mr. Johnson had all the advantages for the forthcoming fall campaign. Republicans-for-Johnson clubs and businessmen-for-Johnson groups formed in several cities without waiting for the Democrats to make official the nomination of Lyndon B. Johnson for President.

The only remaining political uncertainty after the Republicans had chosen in July their presidential team of Barry Goldwater and William Miller was the identity of Mr. Johnson's future running mate. Reporters, sometimes influenced by outsiders, did their best to smoke out Lyndon Johnson on his preference for a vice presidential candidate to join him on the Democratic ticket. The Democratic National Convention was still ahead, scheduled for Atlantic City in the last week of August.

As speculation swirled, and the ambitions of various aspirants to the vice presidential nomination began to be visible in public, President Johnson decided it was time to thin out the potential field.

On July 30, Mr. Johnson held a press conference at the White House and whereas a week earlier he had declined to comment on the vice presidential question at all, this day found him ready. He outlined to the reporters the kind of a vice presidential candidate he desired:

"Among other things, I would like to have a candidate be a man of the people, attractive, prudent, progressive, dedicated to public service, experienced in foreign and domestic affairs, and a man that is well received in all the states of the Union, among all of our people."

This seemed to the reporters to fit any of a number of Democratic leaders but the President denied he had any individual in mind.

About six hours later, reporters were summoned to a conference room near Mr. Johnson's office. The President walked in and read this statement:

"With reference to the selection of the candidate for vice president on the Democratic ticket, I have reached the conclusion that it would be inadvisable for me to recommend to the convention any member of my Cabinet or any of those who meet regularly with the Cabinet.

"In this regard, because their names have been mentioned in the press, I have personally informed the Secretary of State, Mr. Rusk, the Secretary of Defense, Mr. McNamara, the Attorney General, Mr. Kennedy, and the Secretary of Agriculture, Mr. Freeman, of my decision. I have communicated this to the United States Ambassador to the United Nations, Mr. Stevenson, and the head of the Peace Corps, Mr. Shriver.

"In this manner the list has been narrowed. I shall continue to give the most thoughtful consideration to the choice of the man who I will recommend and I shall make my decision known in due course."

Informed sources, said the Associated Press, explained the blockbuster announcement this way: "The President has been working with these men day after day, watching them and the tensions they are under and had decided he did not want to ask any to resign their jobs now to plunge into a political campaign."

Other informed sources saw it as a master stroke on the part of Lyndon B. Johnson in clearing away any possible rivalry to himself in making up the national party ticket and in running the convention show the way he wanted it to go.

In the wake of this swabbing of the decks, speculation about the Democratic vice presidential choice narrowed to Senator Hubert Humphrey and Senator Eugene McCarthy, both of Minnesota. Gone was the speculation about how much leeway would Lyndon Johnson allow in the final choice. Democratic delegates across the nation had been polled and their choice by a 3 to 2 margin was Hubert Humphrey. But President Johnson gave no more hints.

His firm grip on the convention planning had been displayed within the Democratic national committee earlier. The discussion that day centered on housing arrangements for the

50 state delegations and the many others, reporters, workers of all kinds, etc., to be made at Atlantic City. Somebody asked the President where he preferred the Texas delegation to be assigned in the rank of board walk hotels.

"Where had the Massachusetts delegation planned to stay?" he inquired.

This referred, of course, to the early planning done by the late John Kennedy when he picked Atlantic City as the convention site.

"Massachusetts was going to have the Haddon Hall Hotel," said a committeeman.

"Put Texas in the Haddon Hall," said Johnson.

The terse order settled only one fragment of the complicated housing problems at Atlantic City. When Lyndon Johnson detected that the tangle was growing no better rapidly, he called on a young Texas steel company executive to step into the muddle and take it over. This man was Marvin Watson, 40, a wheelhorse in Texas Democratic politics and a decision-maker whose firmness was overlaid with an ingratiating manner. Though the housing for some delegations left quite a bit to be desired compared to the best in the resort center, Marvin Watson did the best he could do for all of them. At least, he evolved a system that erased the original confusion.

To operate the machinery of the convention, President Johnson relied on such stalwarts as David Lawrence of Pennsylvania, Mayor Richard J. Daly of Chicago, Rep. Carl Albert of Oklahoma, Gov. Edmund G. Brown of California, Governor John Connally of Texas, Mayor Robert F. Wagner of New York City, former Gov. Price Daniel of Texas, plus National Chairman John Bailey of Connecticut. Their orders from the White House were to iron out all difficulties in committee meetings so that there would be no floor fights, debates or controversies to expose the inherent divisions within the party.

Walter Jenkins and Cliff Carter manned the presidential command post in a specially-built suite behind the stage of the convention hall. They were the middlemen for President Johnson and his convention leaders.

The control system for sessions of the convention featured a network of telephones connecting chairmen of each delegation with a master phone manned by Cliff Carter behind the speaker's podium. He could talk to each chairman individually, or if need be, talk to all 50 at once. At his side in this electronic hub were television monitor screens giving him views of all vital parts of the huge auditorium. It was the most elaborate communications system ever put together for such a purpose. It meant that from the White House, Lyndon Johnson could be in instant touch with any or all parts of the Democratic convention for whatever purpose he desired.

Through all the hubbub, fanfare and confusion of the convention gathering in Atlantic Ctiy, the speculation ran to new heights on the question of the vice presidential choice. Lyndon Johnson knew this was the only element of suspense available to keep interest in a pageant whose other outcomes were foregone conclusions. He blew gently on the fires. He did nothing to dampen the enthusiasm of backers of Senator McCarthy of Minnesota. The tall, handsome junior senator enjoyed several days in the limelight as a possible nominee.

Then the President sent for Senator Thomas Dodd of Connecticut to fly down to the White House. This started a prairie fire of rumor that the conservative Dodd had been tapped for the national ticket. It was good for a day's feverish gossip up and down the boardwalk.

Finally, President Johnson asked Senator and Mrs. Humphrey to fly down to Washington. The veil was about to part. It was approaching time for the President to appear in Atlantic City. He brought the Humphreys there with him. They landed at the airport just as, miles away in convention hall, Gov. Brown of California was beginning a major speech nominating Lyndon B. Johnson for president. All television coverage at Atlantic City switched to the airport, leaving Brown to speak only to those present in the auditorium. Before the cameras at the airport, Lyndon Johnson made his first announcement that he had chosen Hubert Humphrey as his vice presidential running mate for 1964. The national television audience knew of it at once but the delegates, most of them, in convention hall missed the news.

"Ol' Lyndon scooped himself," said one of the veteran politicians.

The official action came swiftly, once Mr. Johnson and the Humphreys arrived at the hall. Nominated first by John Connally of Texas and then by Gov. Brown of California, Lyndon Johnson accepted in a speech that was heard by (said the networks) 41 million viewers of television:

"Tonight, we of the Democratic Party confidently go before the people offering answers, not retreat—unity, not division —hope, not fear. . . ."

The president called for "rededication to keep burning the golden torch of promise which John F. Kennedy set aflame."

Minutes after accepting the nomination, Lyndon Johnson was back on television, being interviewed on the twin subjects of public opinion polls and the so-called "backlash" of sentiment against racial equality.

"If you really care about lashes," he said, "let's get into this frontlash. Several polls show a backlash of 10 to 15 per cent (against the Democrats because of the new civil rights law) but the same polls show also a frontlash two to three times larger than the backlash . . ."

Eric Sevareid commented: "There's a man who has just made an acceptance speech and he stops to talk about the nuts and bolts of the campaign."

Johnson not only accepted the nomination for himself. He told the delegates of the convention that he recommended they nominate Hubert Humphrey for vice president. Humphrey quickly was nominated and swept the delegates into cheers with a speech ticking off social and economic programs for which both Republicans and Democrats had fought and for which he had voted. After each item, he added, ". . . but not Senator Goldwater." It became a chant. The vast hall rocked with the cheers and chorusing as the delegates joined in the punchline.

So the campaign awaited only the turn of the calendar to go into a September-November hurly burly. The Johnsons and Humphreys flew off to the LBJ Ranch to rest and concoct campaign plans.

Most observers of the political phenomena of 1964 will agree that Lyndon Johnson actually started his presidential campaign in the spring. He left the White House for a series of quick, far-ranging visits to poverty-stricken areas. He walked through drab towns, sat on sagging cabin porches and talked with men, women and children who lived in abject want. It was about the same time that Sargent Shriver, designated by Mr. Johnson as head of the anti-poverty program, unveiled the package of legislative proposals for attacking the problem.

From that period onward, Lyndon Johnson kept himself in the limelight in ways designed to show his concern for people. It was no coincidence that Congress passed, and the President signed, the Economic Opportunity Act late in August.

The Democratic convention gave him another opportunity to dramatize himself as the confident leader of a national party headed for victory in the name of peace, prosperity, prudence, preparedness and justice for all.

His choice of Hubert Humphrey for the vice presidential nomination fit neatly into Mr. Johnson's drive to win the largest election victory in history. Senator Humphrey could match energy, campaign adroitness, idealism, practical political understanding and long experience in national government with the President's own high-geared qualities. Humphrey's closest aides had talent and competence. The Senator and his staff blended without a hitch into the Johnson organization.

According to the calculations of the President and his advisers, his popular appeal would rise in the wake of the extravaganza at Atlantic City, drop off a few points about midway of the ensuing campaign period, then rise to new heights as election day neared. The speaking itineraries for the nominees were geared to this tempo and kept flexible so that tours could be made where current soundings of public opinion indicated the need.

After their post-convention respite at the LBJ ranch in Texas, Johnson and Humphrey hit the campaign trail. The president attracted 100,000 persons to the center of Detroit for a Labor Day speech in which he emphasized the need for a responsible, prudent president in the nuclear age. Humphrey set out through the Middle West, starting in Minnesota, and worked his way to Texas in a fast-moving series of appearances. The juggernaut was rolling.

In retrospect, looking at the unprecedented landslide for Lyndon Johnson that occurred at the polls November 3, it is not easy to remember the uncertainties and qualms of apprehension that beset many, many adherents of his cause from September until the votes were counted. All the indications, before and during the campaign, showed that Johnson would carry nearly all 50 states. The most pessimistic public opinion poll available midway of the campaigning gave him 40 of them. All the other poll gauges showed him favored in 44 states. The crowd response to Lyndon Johnson's far-ranging speaking tours grew in total numbers to record-breaking proportions . . . in Des Moines, in Baltimore, in Los Angeles, through New England and in New Orleans, the turnout of people came in tides called unprecedented by the most expert local observers.

One memory compelled the Democrats and their allies to keep working for a Johnson victory without pause: in 1948, Thomas E. Dewey, the Republican nominee, had been accorded overwhelming victory in advance by public pollsters, and had been defeated soundly at the ballot box by the underdog Democrat, Harry Truman. Overconfidence on the part of Dewey's supporters was widely blamed afterward for the surprise verdict.

Those who opposed the Republican ticket of 1964—whether they believed Senator Goldwater was too reckless, too callous to human needs, or the captive of right wing extremists—gnawed their nails in anxiety until the votes were counted. They were scared stiff at the idea of Goldwater in the White House. It was enough motive to keep them working busily for Johnson and Humphrey.

Feeding this fear was an unprecedented flood of scurrilous printed material castigating Lyndon B. Johnson's character and record. Almost as vicious was the propaganda assault on the patriotism of Hubert Humphrey, whose performance in liberal causes was enough to brand him, in the eyes of ultra-conservatives, as suspect. Similar smears on Senator Goldwater through paperback "books" never achieved the multi-million-copy circulation of those aimed at Lyndon Johnson.

So cleverly done, so glibly assertive and so widely circulated were these paperbacks and tabloid "newspaper" throwaways that their possible effects caused worry among many Democratic adherents. This worry spread despite the fact that knowledgeable critics punctured their contents quickly. Read carefully by any reasonable person with any knowledge of the facts, these smears could be classified for what they were: paranoid half-truths and lies concocted in an absurd brew. The hatred in every paragraph repelled more readers than the mishmash of claims and accusations deceived, if the election returns are any gauge of their impact on the campaign.

In a different category entirely, but equally as unsettling to some Johnson partisans, was the sudden publication of detailed discussions of the Johnson family's business and personal fortunes. The thought behind this newspaper and magazine investigation was that Lyndon Johnson's long tenure in Washington made it possible for the broadcasting business owned by his wife to prosper through LBJ's influence on the Federal Communications Commission. After the most diligent and exhaustive search of the records of the FCC and the Johnson corporate structure, no evidence of misdeeds was found, although there was ample evidence that Mr. and Mrs. Johnson knew how to make their holdings increase in value through canny management, sharp trading and sound investment. The journalistic exercise in Johnson family economics ended with an assertion by one national publication that their total net worth was $14 millions, and a report from the accounting firm that handles the Johnson enterprises' records that the net worth was a little more than $3 millions. This led in turn to publication of the estimated financial standings of the other candidates, showing that Senator Goldwater was a millionaire, Representative Miller was moderately well off and Senator Humphrey worth less than $200,000. The whole sequence held the public eye for a brief time during the campaign.

During Lyndon Johnson's years as Democratic leader in the U.S. Senate, his most effective servant was the secretary to the majority, Robert Baker. This young South Carolinian had worked his way from a Senate page boy's job into the influential staff position by an unusual talent for ingratiating himself with senators, especially those who found his energy, his quick intelligence and his all-knowing fund of information useful to themselves.

Lyndon Johnson not only used Bobby Baker to the fullest in dominating the Senate; he praised him publicly as "the most tireless and indefatigable man" connected with the Senate. Johnson also met Baker's father in South Carolina during the 1960 campaign and told him that Bobby Baker was "my strong right arm, the last man I see at night, the first one I see in the morning."

Their association ended when Lyndon Johnson was elected Vice President, for his constitutional duty of presiding over the Senate entailed no more opportunity to control the Democratic members. Baker continued as secretary to the majority.

In September, 1963, a business associate of Baker's brought suit against him over the details of a vending machine company they had created. The action unloosed a Pandora's box of charges, allegations and stories about the extra-curricular activities of Bobby Baker. Most of them had to do with high-flying business transactions in which he and various senators and a mixed group of outsiders were involved. There was also much talk about party girls, lavish entertainment and other hijinks as part of some of these transactions. Public disclosures and gossip about the Bobby Baker case, as it came to be known, were building to a high pitch when John Kennedy was slain and Lyndon Johnson became President of the United States.

A committee of the Senate began an investigation on the strength of some of the accusations against Baker. One witness revealed that he had given a stereophonic radio costing more than $500 to Lyndon Johnson at the urging of Bobby Baker. President Johnson told reporters that it was a personal gift from Baker to the Johnson family, and added that the two families had exchanged gifts for years.

The Senate committee met often in the spring of 1964, recessed its inquiry for months, and finally ended, presumably, its investigations in the early months of 1965 without having resolved the many conflicts in testimony it had received. Baker himself declined to answer all questions.

No criminal actions had been proved against him, either in the Senate hearings or in grand jury investigation.

The case found a juicy place in Republican charges against the Democrats, and against Lyndon Johnson, during the 1964 election campaign but nothing definitive came of it.

Another spectacular story, arising from the bankruptcy of Billie Sol Estes, young Texas chemical fertilizer tycoon, who had courted prominent Democrats on his way to a paper fortune, furnished much grist for the gossip mill of Republican partisans. Many efforts were made to link Estes with Lyndon B. Johnson but all came to naught. What most of those who sought this link didn't realize was that Estes and Johnson had been on opposite sides of the long Texas Democratic conflict; that there not only wasn't any tie between them, there was no mutual regard at any time.

The most incredible episode of the period came when Walter Jenkins, for 25 years the most trusted confidante of Lyndon B. Johnson and the aide who ran the White House for him, was accused by the Washington police department's morals squad of an indecent act with an older man. When this incident became known to President Johnson simultaneously with its publication, he asked and received Jenkins' resignation. But it was a triple blow to the President. The two men and their families were the most intimate of friends. Walter Jenkins was an officer in the Johnson company until it went into trusteeship in late 1963. He had worked, for 25 years, around the clock for Johnson in politics, government and business. He was a devout and honored Roman Catholic; devoted to his wife and their six children. For months he had been the concern of his physician because of the effects of too-long hours, too much strain and too little rest in his key position at the White House. When the morals case broke, so did Walter Jenkins. He went to a hospital for a long period of treatment and rest.

Efforts to inject the Jenkins case into the presidential campaign came to naught for a variety of reasons. Senator Goldwater himself forbade it from his standpoint. As a Major General in Air Force Reserve, Barry Goldwater was Col. Walter Jenkins' commanding officer in the 9999th AF Reserve Squadron. He knew how selfless and dedicated a public servant was this man.

So did everybody else in Washington who knew Walter Jenkins, and they numbered nearly everybody in the top ranks of both political parties. He had near-unanimous sympathy in and out of the government. A group of clergymen published a strong warning against making the personal tragedy of Walter Jenkins an issue in the electioneering.

More than anything else, however, the thunder of international events swept aside the domestic concerns represented by scurrilous propaganda, candidates' financial ratings and Mr. Jenkins. Nikita Khrushchev was deposed in a sudden overturn of the Soviet Union's top leadership, and the scientists of Communist China exploded their first atomic device. The Soviet space experts also orbited a three-man space vehicle to demonstrate again their superiority to the United States in manned space flight capability.

These mid-October reminders that world dangers not only existed but possibly might become more acute at any moment brought a different mood to the electorate. The drumfire of personal attacks on Lyndon Johnson no longer had much significance compared to his awesome responsibilities in the face of new unknowns in the Communist world. The President and those campaigning for him played to the hilt the proved talents of the man in the White House: calmness, courage, prudence, determination.

Two weeks later the landslide became official. Lyndon Johnson received more votes and won a higher percentage of the votes than any previous candidate for president. He carried sections of the country where Democrats seldom or never had won before to an extent unheard-of in the past. He was the first candidate of any kind to carry all the counties in the State of New York. He swept all the states except for five in the South and Senator Goldwater's own Arizona.

Yet Lyndon Johnson's mood as he watched election returns on television at a series of parties in Austin on the night of November 3, 1964, was a mixture of jubilation and gravity. He called the results "a victory for unity." He sounded the theme of good will to all Americans. He remembered the vivid demonstrations of hatred that popped up in some campaign crowds, and read in the returns from Dixie how far from a solution was the bitter racial strife. If he had won the biggest election victory in history, he knew also that the people would expect him to work miracles on their behalf, and he knew that miracles of the sort demanded were not likely to happen. He hoped that the vote of confidence would produce a national feeling sufficient to win for him extra time to work at the monumental problems of the presidency.

The winner seemed assured of a second honeymoon for at least a while if all the newspapers that had supported him for election stood by him now. Nearly all of the major metropolitan dailies, including many that never before had endorsed a Democrat for president, and most of the magazines that took a position, had exhorted the voters on behalf of Lyndon Johnson. Most of them did so, they said, because of his performance after November 22, 1963. And they added that his opponent couldn't match Johnson's capabilities for the presidency.

His landslide also produced large Democratic majorities in Congress, and enhanced the Democratic party in state and local offices across most of the nation.

But the international horizons were dark in Southeast Asia, Africa, the Far East, and, economically, in Europe. If Lyndon Johnson had been treading water on international problems, as one observer said, the time was near when he'd have to strike out and swim.

Again Lyndon Johnson and Hubert Humphrey met at the LBJ ranch, this time to assess the work ahead in Congress and in the complex world beyond the U.S. borders. Their period of relaxation was short.

In the next few weeks, President Johnson grappled anew with a federal budget which he barely held under $100 billions, with his State of the Union message, with the results of 14 or 15 task forces who had been working at his request for months on domestic programs for the future and with the unpredictable complications of world affairs. He also had to reorganize his White House staff, and there was his inauguration ceremony and celebration in the near offing.

In planning the latter occasion, Johnson handed over to a committee the intricate and vexing work of arranging inaugural balls to follow the oath-taking. But he supervised the details of the ceremony and parade himself, down to timing in advance the prayers to be offered by four clergymen. He scheduled an early church service to precede the inauguration. He invited the great Mormon Tabernacle Choir to sing at the swearing-in exercises. He managed his own inaugural address in such a manner as to project a consistent theme of solemnity and reverence that will be remembered long by those who attended the affair in front of the capital.

The president set a tone for his next four years even before he took the oath of office. In a State of the Union message that carried broad import of firmness in world affairs along with a hope for peace, and sketched an outline of his Great Society ambitions, he also said this:

"The greatest burden (of the presidency) is not running the huge operations of government—or meeting daily troubles, large and small—or even working with the Congress.

131

"A President's hardest task is not to do what is right, but to know what is right.

"Yet the presidency brings no special gift of prophecy or foresight. You take an oath—step into an office—and must then help guide a great democracy.

"The answer was waiting for me in the land where I was born.

"It was once barren land. The angular hills were covered with scrub cedar and a few live oaks. Little would grow in the harsh caliche soil. And each spring, the Pedernales River would flood the valley.

"But men came and worked and endured and built.

"Today that country is abundant with fruit, cattle, goats and sheep. There are pleasant homes, and lakes, and the floods are gone.

"Why did men come to that once forbidding land?

"They were restless, of course, and had to be moving on. But there was more than that. There was a dream—a dream of a place where a free man could build for himself, and raise his children to a better life—a dream of a continent to be conquered, a world to be won, a nation to be made.

"A president does not shape a new and personal vision of America. He collects it from the scattered hopes of the American past. It existed when the first settlers saw the coast of a new world, and when the first pioneers moved westward. It has guided us every step of the way.

"It sustains every president. But it is also your inheritance and it belongs equally to the people we serve.

"It must be interpreted anew by each generation for its own needs; as I have tried, in part, to do today. It shall lead us as we enter this third century of the search for a 'more perfect union.'

"This, then, is the State of the Union: free, restless, growing and full of hope.

"So it was in the beginning.

"So it shall always be, while God is willing, and we are strong enough to keep the faith."

Sixteen days later, as tens of thousands of citizens stood in the thin snow of Capitol Hill in Washington, and millions of others watched on television, Lyndon Baines Johnson stood before the Chief Justice to take his oath of office.

In a typical last-minute Johnson touch, he had Mrs. Johnson hold the Bible on which he rested his hand. At his request, she stepped forward to do this in place of the Senate aide who had been assigned to hold the book.

After repeating the solemn words, President Johnson began

132

in a slow, measured voice to deliver his inaugural address. He promised to lead the nation to a destiny of justice, liberty and union. And he predicted that before this generation ends, it will see the conquest of poverty, hunger, ignorance and discrimination.

He added, "I will lead as best I can. But look within your own hearts—to the old promises and the old dream. They will lead you best of all."

President Johnson said his Great Society is not to be "the ordered changeless and sterile battalion of the ants."

"It is the excitement of becoming—always becoming, trying, probing, falling, resting, and trying again—but always gaining . . .

"If the nation succeeds, it will be not because of what we have, but what we are; not because of what we own, but what we believe . . .

"We believe every man must someday be free, and we believe in ourselves," he intoned.

The President said the time has come for the United States to achieve progress without strife and change without hatred.

"Let us reject any among us who seek to reopen old wounds and rekindle old hatreds. They stand in the way of a seeking nation . . ."

After a luncheon for the Johnsons and the Humphreys, the official party took seats in a heated viewing stand in front of the White House to watch a parade of bands, marching units, floats and dancing girls. This, too, had the Johnson touch: the number of its units was restricted by his order to the point that all its elements could pass in review before darkness fell. Each state, except Texas, was limited to one marching band. Texas had two: the University of Texas Longhorn band and the San Marcos State College band.

The last business of the day was pleasure, for those of stamina and determination. Five inaugural balls for celebrating Democrats at five different locations in Washington brought out thousands of men and women in formal dress.

President and Mrs. Johnson and their two daughters visited every one of the five ballrooms. The president danced at each one. At the last one on his itinerary, in the Sheraton Park Hotel, he quipped to the crowd: "Never have so many paid so much to dance so little." The couples jammed together on the huge floor left little room for dancing, but they made room for a swinging, swooping presidential couple.

The gala events of the inauguration ended a hectic year for Mrs. Johnson, Lynda and Luci. They carried a man's share of the political burden for President Johnson through spring, summer and fall of 1964. Sometimes they accompanied him on speaking tours. But as often, if not more so, they went on their own speaking assignments. The girls usually appeared singly, since their school routines were different.

Mrs. Johnson often went alone on journeys to make speeches, preside at ceremonies and visit faithful party worker gatherings. Her most memorable contribution to the election campaign was her own "whistle stop" train tour of 1600 miles through eight Southern states. From the observation car platform of the train and at rallies indoors and outdoors along the route, she urged the audiences to work and vote for Lyndon Johnson and Hubert Humphrey. Always smiling, always courteous, she bore up to a grinding schedule of speaking and handshaking that would have taxed a far stronger person.

Political observers said afterwards that Mrs. Johnson's train trip revived Democratic support in an important way just at the time when it was sagging in the states she visited. The fact that the Democrats carried Virginia, North Carolina and Florida was attributed in no small measure to Mrs. Johnson's persuasive efforts during her "whistle stop" tour.

CHAPTER XIV

When Lyndon Johnson took the oath of office as President of the United States in the airplane at Dallas on November 22, 1963, it seemed to dawn on nearly all who knew anything about our government that here was the best-prepared President in American history.

This chronicle has traced his preparation, his march up the steps of public service to the pinnacle. And yet, so complex is the personality of Lyndon Johnson, and so broad-ranging has been his active life, that no single chronicle can capture the full image of the man.

Essentially, he is action personified. Yet he acts only after the fullest preparation.

Masculine in the fullest sense, he can be tender and affectionate.

Perfectionist in all things, he can appear gay and carefree.

By turns imperious, cajoling, cool and dignified, as exuberant as a cheer leader, brusque and demanding, Lyndon Johnson exudes vitality in every mood, every gesture.

The man's sensitivity to others runs much deeper than what has been described in him as vanity. He wants everybody to like him, to admire him, but he also tries to return the feeling full measure. As a consequence, he finds friendships over a wide range of humanity.

John B. Connally, his friend and fellow worker in politics since 1938, says of Lyndon Johnson: "He will have a human instinct that will surpass any other person you will ever encounter. He is a person of great charm and great poise . . . always determined, always firm, always a man of his convictions, an indomitable and indefatigable worker, working always for perfection."

Connally's experience at Johnson's side includes working in his congressional office, helping to manage political campaigns, helping to manage political conventions. They have much more in common. Both of them are farm and ranch bred. They swap information on their own ranches today. Johnson listened to John Connally boast about the Connally ranch's coastal Bermuda grass pastures and had Connally supervise the planting of a pasture in the same grass on the LBJ Ranch.

Yet their closeness and mutual admiration have not prevented their taking differing stands on some public questions. Connally's independence is another of his traits respected by Lyndon Johnson.

Johnson's attraction to strong and capable men who admire his capacities is a hallmark of his public career. Some of these men are known in politics, others in the world of letters, and some are successful private citizens, mostly business executives.

Dean Acheson came to know young Senator Johnson during the Truman Administration and went on record in these words spoken to a reporter in 1960 summing up the then hopeful presidential aspirant:

"I'm an admirer of Senator Johnson. Politics is one of the greatest arts, one of the most difficult arts, one of the most obscure arts. It does not necessarily flower from high and ancient cultures—France, Germany, the Italians. There are damn few places where it does—Britain and some of the English-speaking nations, the United States.

"It's the incredibly difficult task of getting things done. How in the world do you get your fellow citizens around to the point where they will do something?"

Politics, he said, "is a high gift; democracy is almost a self-made obstacle race. Therefore, when somebody can operate this sort of thing, as Franklin Roosevelt could do, as Lyndon Johnson can do—this excites my admiration."

Discussing Lyndon Johnson's achievements in the Senate in the broadest terms, Acheson said:

"He has taken an institution which in its organization and by its history has almost been created to be inefficient, and has made it work. Congress and particularly the Senate historically has been organized by putting all its powers in the committee—almost for government by unanimous consent, or no government . . . he's made the darn thing work."

Acheson said he worked with Johnson very closely on civil rights. Speaking of the 1957 Act, he said, "The only civil rights law we've had since the Civil War was passed in the Senate by Senator Johnson. It is customary to say the 1957 Act was a bad bill because Title III, to give the Attorney General injunctive powers, was knocked out of it. Johnson led the effort to remove it, as he did again in 1960. That was a damn fool article anyway. It would have caused endless litigation as to what it would have meant. It picked up all the vague clauses of the Reconstruction Acts and made them enforceable by the Attorney General."

As for Johnson's opposition to restriction of the filibuster rules of the Senate, Acheson said, "This is the judgment of a man who has an instinct for government." If he had all the votes in the country, Acheson said, he "would put Lyndon Johnson in the White House. . . ."

"There is a whole side of this man which I think is not known and is not appreciated in the public man. He has thought about a great many things since his illness [the heart attack in 1955]. He has a side which is contemplative and wise and tender and really deep. . . . He is very cagey. He is very cocky. He gives the impression that he knows all the answers—that he knows all this. This is not the case at all. I think it's true there is a strong element of vanity. I say vanity, not conceit. I think he has a very proud nature, and he doesn't like people prying around—and I understand this. . . .

"He stands for the greatest thing in the world, and that is to keep this organized society going, and in the right direction. It's fine to be liberal, fine to have ideas, fine to shout your mouth off all the time. But he has got to get Harry Byrd and Wayne Morse to do the same thing, and that's very hard to do. Johnson is a man who really has some idea about what he wants to do with the country and knows how to do it. I've talked about his ability to get hold of things quickly. I think he does understand the importance of power . . . he's quite able to learn about anything.

"Great rounded sentences? He wouldn't get far in that competition. He would say here are some of the problems in the terms of possibilities—better opportunities for children—whether you call it liberalism or what, these are the problems: farm income, urban redevelopment, school problems, taxation—these are the things that you do. . . ."

Lyndon Johnson can't resist reading a newspaper or watching, whenever he can, a television news program. His avid interest goes beyond the information offered. He wants to see how the news is treated, what is emphasized, what is skimmed over or omitted, and what opinions, editorial or otherwise, are on view.

News people fascinate Johnson, too, individually and as a group. As in all public figures, he understands and appreciates some news reporters more than he does others. He resents prying questions, and in a man of Johnson's nature, the possibility of his considering a question prying is higher than usual. He has been known to upbraid reporters for something they wrote. His complaint sometimes has been that their stories were inaccurate, at other times that they were unfair. In this tenderness, his anatomy is characteristic of most public men.

From the time Mrs. Johnson's television station began operating, her husband has had close contact with TV executives and production people. Some of them he considers close friends. He is a critical student of the news formats and news ideas in television, has been known to offer suggestions that resulted in better programs.

Lyndon Johnson's fascination for the press, and with the press, stems surely in part from his parental roots. His mother was a newspaper reporter, and so was her father, in addition to being an editor himself. Lyndon Johnson was a campus editor at San Marcos State College. One of his earliest and most enduring friendships in Washington dates from 1933 when Johnson was assistant to Congressman Richard Kleberg and William S. White, formerly of the Austin American, was an Associated Press reporter covering the House of Representatives. Mrs. Johnson holds a degree in journalism from the University of Texas. She and her husband almost went into the newspaper business after she received her first inheritance, and again only recently seriously considered trying to buy an historic daily newspaper in Texas.

But more than all this, or perhaps added atop all this, Lyndon Johnson has been a newsmaker in his own right for 30 years and consequently has been the subject of newspaper reporters at every level—local, state, national and international. Not only to see his own name in print, but to see other names, and accounts of deeds and ideas and events, Lyndon Johnson had always been an avid newspaper reader. From the time his own name began to appear in the press, he has been a critical newspaper reader. And from the time he figured out who was the boss of the reporter, he has been a newspaper reader who got in touch with editors and publishers.

Like any man of active political life, Lyndon Johnson upon occasion has tried to shun or avoid the press, and perhaps more often, has tried to cultivate better relations with the reporters and editors and publishers.

Johnson has had only occasional success with each of these courses.

During his years in the U.S. Senate, especially, Lyndon Johnson sought out reporters for important Eastern newspapers. In part he wanted a better national portrayal of his own activities, but equally as much wanted a less parochial view of his section of the United States, the Southwest, and in particular, Texas. In this he had limited success, but he did win the personal admiration of a number of reporters whose knowledge of the Senate caused them to appreciate the genius with which Senate Majority Leader Johnson went about his duties.

More than one writer has described the "Johnson treatment" of those days. The senator would draw a reporter into a secluded spot, exhort, explain, pat his knee, pull his lapels, stab his chest with a forefinger, wrap an arm around his shoulder, thrust the Johnson face close to the writer's own, lament, cajole and demand . . . all in a breathtaking sequence of monologue that left the subject wrung out, mentally more than physically. Sometimes the senator won his objective. Always he engraved himself on another's memory forever.

When Lyndon Johnson became president, and after he had put the suddenly-obtained office in reasonable order, he turned his attention to the matter of dealing with the White House reporters. He had never thought much of the tele-vised, formal "press conference" where a few reporters popped laborious questions at the President, who could an-swer in a quip, an evasive tangle of syntax, or a pre-cooked paragraph . . . then quickly pick another questioner. These performances, it had seemed to Vice President Johnson, were only fair entertainment and almost zero as far as exchanging ideas or information went.

Early in December, 1963, President Johnson without warn-ing called the available White House reporters into his office for coffee and a chat. It was his first press conference as presi-dent. The reporters crowded around his desk as they once did around Franklin D. Roosevelt's. It was an informal exercise. Repeatedly in the following weeks, President Johnson sprang his experimental press conference without advance notice. Nearly always he did it on a Saturday. This obtained for him page one treatment in the major Sunday newspapers. It also complicated the lives of the reporters. At first, it was mainly relief men or second string Saturday personnel who partici-pated. But this was only Phase I.

One Saturday, President Johnson essayed a full-dress White House televised press conference, and brought it off neatly. Again, in April, he had an even larger televised press con-ference, for the first and only time in the State Department auditorium where Mr. Kennedy had held forth so often.

As the weather warmed up, the President took to calling reporters to join him in a walk around the White House grounds, with an invitation to ask him questions. He could walk faster and talk in lower tones and absolutely bumfuzzle his reporter companions when he chose to do it, and he occasionally did.

During the spring and summer of 1964, President Johnson

in one way or another had press conferences at frequent intervals at the White House. In one period, he had one a day for three consecutive days.

Then he'd take off for the LBJ Ranch, with the accompanying press plane bearing 50 or 60 or more reporters to stay in Texas. The difficulty was that he stayed on the ranch and they stayed 65 miles away at Austin. Occasionally, he invited them to the ranch, which meant a chartered bus ride, round trip, of 130 miles before they could report a word. As often, the White House press would have to be content with a mass interview of the presidential press secretary—variously, Pierre Salinger, Malcolm Kilduff, or George Reedy—in a ballroom on the mezzanine floor of the Driskill Hotel. Sometimes there was news involved, sometimes mostly a semi-serious heckling of the press secretary.

After his election as President, and as world problems beset him more seriously than before, Mr. Johnson saw the press at less and less frequent intervals. From a time when he was calling press conferences several times a week, he went to the other extreme of not having such a conference for weeks on end. The reporters began to spend much of their time writing critical articles about the President's failure to meet with them.

In short, after 30 years of trying, Lyndon Johnson has not yet found a way to satisfy the demands of all newspaper reporters, and doubtless never will.

But the President uses selected reporters frequently, the ones on whom he can depend to follow his ground rules as to attribution, quotation, background only, or clues for finding a story somewhere else that the President thinks should be found. These private press conferences are useful to him, and to the reporters involved.

The President also has emerged as an effective television speaker and nobody is more surprised at this than himself. For years he shunned television as not suited to his style of talk and appearance. But as in so many other instances, once he set out to master it, master it he did.

And the flow of news from the White House, whether from the President himself or from his press spokesman, has never been more voluminous. The President wants to communicate with people, but wants it done his way.

Johnson searches for ability and energy and imagination wherever he can find them and put them to work. In 1958 he added to his staff as personal assistant Bill Moyers, then in his early twenties, and kept him close by his side until 1961. Moyers then became deputy director of the Peace

Corps and seems destined to go much higher in public administration. When Johnson became Vice President, he persuaded the late Dr. Walter Prescott Webb, elderly and much-honored historian, to join the Johnson staff to enrich the Vice President's thinking on problems relating to the interplay of populations, land and water.

Johnson has cultivated a friendship with Dr. J. Frank Dobie, best-known of the Southwestern folklorists. He has woven warm relations with such scientist-managers as David Sarnoff and Admiral Hyman Rickover.

Lyndon Johnson's interests range over the entire national scene. He instinctively had this broad scope of mind. He has cultivated it steadily from the time he first entered public life in 1931.

But the same Lyndon Johnson is as keenly interested in the minutest details of his own offices, his ranch, and Mrs. Johnson's business enterprises. He advises freely on the personal appearance of his staff members down to such details as the knots in their neckties and the color combinations of the women's clothing . . . and their waistlines.

So much has been written in recent years about Johnson's tailoring and cuff links and fondness for putting the LBJ initials on everything that he is likely now to say, "This suit only cost eighty dollars, but they keep writing about my two-hundred-dollar suits." His personal appearance is always correctly conservative unless he thinks the occasion calls for Western regalia, in which case he wears cowboy garb with a true flair of authenticity. But he is just as likely to don an Ivy League cap, or even a French beret, when he heads outdoors to ride in his auto or his motorboat.

The cowboy hat is required in Texas politics. Constables, Supreme Court judges, members of the legislature, and every other grade of political office holder in Texas wears the beige Western hat . . . some have thought in order to be distinguished from the voters. For years, Lyndon Johnson followed the custom, and still keeps several broad-brimmed hats in his closet. But since the late 1950's he is usually seen wearing an ordinary business hat, or even bareheaded.

Lyndon Johnson seldom wears a topcoat. On the ranch, depending on the season, he likes a khaki jacket or a short leather jacket. His metabolism enables him to wear nothing heavier than a medium weight suit unless the weather is extremely cold. In good weather, beside his swimming pool or on the motorboat, Johnson favors shorts and a tropical short-sleeved shirt—or no shirt at all. Sun and sleep are his two favorite prescriptions for relaxation.

With the rising fortunes of the Johnson business interests beginning in the mid-1950's, Mr. Johnson has found it increasingly possible to indulge one of his best-loved hobbies —shopping—and to follow his open-handed sense of generosity of giving away clothing, watches, cigarette lighters, paintings, and other goods he may buy in the course of a shopping visit.

During his tour of Scandinavia in the fall of 1963, the official functions requiring Johnson's presence kept him from attending a fashion show which the hosts arranged for Mrs. Johnson, their daughter, and women aides. He was so disappointed at not seeing the style display that those who staged it brought most of the models and clothing to the Johnson suite for a private showing. He bought a number of dresses and other clothes, most of which he gave to friends upon his return home.

In possession of the LBJ Ranch only a dozen years, the Johnsons have so implanted their personalties on it that it is difficult to imagine them without the ranch, or the ranch without the Johnsons.

When they traded the former Sam Johnson residence in Johnson City to Mrs. Clarence Martin, who was Lyndon Johnson's father's sister—Aunt Frank—Lyndon and Lady Bird Johnson faced the decision of wrecking the dilapidated ranch house or trying to make it over into a habitable dwelling. The old stone portion was so soundly built that they decided on a restoration.

They generally followed the original floor scheme to rebuild a plain, roomy, but not spacious, country-style ranch house of two stories. It wasn't luxurious then nor is it now. Mr. and Mrs. Johnson's tastes run to comfort rather than to luxury. At the time Lyndon Johnson came there for convalescence in 1955, the ranch house and barn, with about 230 acres of land, constituted the main facilities.

Probably the first improvement, after the house itself, had been the construction of a low-water channel dam on the shallow Pedernales River as it runs across the front of the property. This concrete dam impounds a pool 200 yards long. The road crossing the river to reach the house runs on a concrete shelf in front of the dam. The normal flow of water over the dam keeps a few inches of water spilling across the roadway. This add an extra fillip to the task of driving across the stream. In time of high water it blocks the road, so that an approach must be made from another direction.

A rural road parallels the Pedernales on the side across from the ranch buildings. Motorists using that road have a panoramic view of the house and other features—the white fences, the barns, live oaks, lawn, and shrubbery.

Shortly after Johnson's heart attack, friends gave to the LBJ Ranch a steel flagpole set in concrete just outside the fence in front of the swimming pool. When Senator Johnson was at the ranch, the flags flew in this order: at the top, the Stars and Stripes; next below, the Lone Star flag of Texas; at the third rank, a blue flag with the initials LBJ. After he became vice president Johnson substituted the vice presidential penant for the LBJ flag. Now he flies only the Stars and Stripes and the presidential flag.

A unique Johnson guest register is the custom of having visitors sign their names and the date on a freshly poured concrete block. These are then used, when cured, to make steppingstones through the thick lawn around the house. Some of the most famous names in the world, as well as some obscure Texas names, decorate these flagstones at the LBJ.

First new addition to the LBJ's comforts after Mr. Johnson's recovery was the swimming pool, complete with heating equipment so that it can be used year round, and a bath house. A thick carpet-grass lawn came next. Later demands for extra room brought the building of a modern office attached to the house, the construction of a six-bedroom frame guest house, and an enlarged dining room. The upstairs bedrooms were refinished with new furniture and baths in yellow, ivory, and green. The window-unit air conditioners first used have given way to a central system of cooling and heating. The evolution of the LBJ accommodations, in short, has been gradual, reflecting Mr. Johnson's rise in national responsibility and Mrs. Johnson's rise as a successful businesswoman.

In 1952 a flood ripped through the valley of the Pedernales, uprooting trees, washing away fences and some buildings. The LBJ Ranch structures are safely above flood level, but for days in that deluge the ranch was cut off from all outside contact by the raging torrent. Senator Johnson was in Austin and Mrs. Johnson was marooned at the ranch. He chartered a light airplane which managed to land in the field behind the house so he could be at her side.

From the time of that landing, the LBJ has gradually become an aviation center. First came a grassy strip for light planes, then a graveled strip, than an asphalt runway of 3,000 feet, and now a thicker asphalt runway of 6,300 feet stretching up the slope behind the buildings. A sheet-metal building serves as a combination hanger, hay barn, implement shed, and storage room.

In the fall of 1963, visiting the ranch, Lyndon Johnson noticed that a stack of lumber had been placed in the hangar portion of the sheet-metal structure. He asked his young ranch foreman whether he thought it proper to block out the airplane from its shelter.

"Oh, it won't take ten minutes to move the lumber to make room for the airplane," said the foreman.

"You get those two other fellows and move it," said Johnson dryly, "and I'm going to time you." He drove off to a pasture and was back in fifteen minutes. The lumber had been shifted. "How long did it take you to move it?" Johnson asked.

"Ten minutes," said the foreman, grinning.

When he is at the ranch, Johnson gives the foreman and other employees the same supervision that he is famous for using on his office staffs. He wants exact answers to all his questions about crops, pastures, cattle, and the use of the irrigation pumps and pipes that carry water from the pool on the Pedernales to his pastures.

On a thirty-minute auto ride with the foreman one evening, Johnson cross-examined him on their cattle-breeding practices. Mr. Johnson started the debate when he said the head of the Southwestern Cattle Raisers Association had advised him to cross his Hereford cows with a Devon bull so that the calves would grow larger, faster. The young foreman, trained at Texas A. and M. College on strict purebred cattle procedures, had many objections to crossbreeding. Johnson questioned each objection, wanted facts. A few days later he shipped a Devon bull to the LBJ.

When Mr. Johnson is in residence, or even on a flying visit, at the LBJ, he goes out in the morning and again in the evening to look at the Hereford cattle grazing on the several pastures. Standard equipment on his air-conditioned sedan is a special horn that imitates the bellow of a bull. His well-fed, placid cattle are so accustomed to being visited by automobile that they seldom rise, if lying down, or move more than a step or two at his approach—until he hits the bull-horn button. Then he sets them in motion. He wants to see them moving so he can judge their condition.

While deer hunting in Texas goes on only during the final six weeks of the year, Lyndon Johnson enjoys going out after sundown to watch the deer at night any time of the year. He drives his high-priced sedan over the pastures as if it were a jeep, looking for the glint of deer eyes ahead of the light beams. The hill country has a full population of deer, and also a big supply of "varmints" such as foxes, ringtail cats, skunks, oppossum—and Mr. Johnson takes a census of those, too, as his headlights reveal their lurking presence.

On the LBJ, which now has grown to more than 400 acres, and on nearby leased pasturage, Lyndon Johnson provides plenty of grass, some grain and water to attract deer and keep them healthy. He hunts nearly every day of the season when he is on the ranch, has escorted many guests out to shoot their buck, but he shows as much excitement over the sight of a running bunch of deer as in shooting at them. And he wants to share the scene with anybody who will ride the pastures with him.

Lyndon and Lady Bird Johnson share themselves and their ranch for wider purposes. He has more of the blood of his missionary forebearers. When the Johnsons can bring international guests to the ranch, they take pains to invite Texans to come out and share a meal and conversation, and thus become better acquainted with people from afar.

One notable occasion in 1963 saw thirty-one United Nations delegates flown to the LBJ for a full day of feasting and Western-style entertainment interspersed with personal visiting by about two hundred Texans from nearby cities and ranches. The program was almost the same as the one planned for Mr. and Mrs. Kennedy on the visit so tragically prevented.

For the Asians, Europeans and Africans in the United Nations party at the LBJ, the Johnsons presented a comedy hillbilly band, a trick pistol-shot artist of the Texas Department of Public Safety, a troupe of trained dogs, and a bull-whip expert—all performing in turn on the grassy banks of the Pedernales below and in front of the ranch house.

Then Lyndon Johnson rose and bade his guests to feel entirely welcome because, he said, the international flavor has always been strong in these hills. "When I first went to Congress in 1937, newspapers were published in this district in ten languages—German, Czech, Polish, Swedish, Spanish, Arabic and English, as well as Democratic, Republican and Texan. . . .

"What men have achieved here and all through our land reflects not the special talents of a special breed, but the influence, we believe, of the special gift of individaul freedom. . . ."

The whole atmosphere that day, over barbecued steaks and much conversation, reflected the person-to-person acquaintance that is a Johnson specialty.

J. Frank Dobie watching the proceedings that day, recalled the camel driver's visit to the LBJ ranch because it showed, he said, how Lyndon Johnson is able to be at complete ease with every kind of person. "He has respect for human beings and sympathy for them. He has no awe of people in high places nor comtempt for those in lower stations.

"I was there that day at the ranch. I doubt if Lyndon Johnson ever had a better time in his life. I know I never did. The camel driver was as much at ease as if he were talking with another camel driver in Pakistan. And it was all Lyndon's doing. Not everybody can do that."

Ever since his coronary illness, Lyndon Johnson has struggled with the diet problem. For a year or two after his recovery, he managed to keep his weight near the 180 to 185 pounds urged by doctors. But in later years, his fondness for hearty food had added extra pounds, mostly at the waistline. Like many another diet-conscious American, he occasionally goes on a rigid fast—say, skipping breakfast, little or no lunch—then at dinner enjoys a rich beef menu topped with an honest dessert. He's an icebox prowler, too, when he comes into the ranch kitchen late at night. A cold pork chop, a hunk of venison sausage, a slab of homemade bread —these he finds hard to resist.

The guests who eat breakfast, brunch, lunch or dinner at the LBJ never lack for delicious food. The bacon and hams are from LBJ porkers, cured at the Johnson City locker plant. Venison is a favorite item from the freezer. The menu may include beef in any of its known forms, home-canned vegetables and fruit; hot breads; and for those who like them, including Lyndon B. Johnson, a bowl of jalapeno peppers still shining from the sesame oil and spices packed with them in Mexico.

Since the Johnsons began their custom of entertaining notables from abroad at the LBJ, the neighbors in the vicinity have taken a personal interest in helping with the hospitality. The nearby village of Stonewall calls itself the "peach capital of the world." LBJ neighbors bring baskets of fruit, jars of preserves, jams, jellies and home-prepared vegetables to the ranch kitchen when they hear that the Johnsons are coming with distinguished guests.

"This is something they do without being asked," says a staff member. "They are proud of the reputation for hospitality in the hill country."

About the time Lyndon Johnson became Vice President, Mrs. Johnson acquired a tract of lake front property fifty miles northeast of the LBJ Ranch, on the Llano River, where one of the lakes created through the work of Johnson many years before makes a hill country resort area. Starting late,

Lyndon Johnson became enamored of motorboating and lakeside living. At the same time, he found a radio-telephone relay system that could serve the Johnsons on a multi-unit hookup linking Austin, the LBJ, the lakeside house, the motorboat, and their personal airplane.

With his urgent desire to be in touch with everybody all the time, Lyndon Johnson ever since has kept the air waves crackling in the triangular area of the Texas hills.

On the radio telephone network now, the Johnsons can coordinate guests coming from Austin, or a party moving from the ranch to the lake, or vice versa, with instant intercommunication at all times.

The cook at the ranch, for example, is now expert in using the radio. She receives instructions as to menu and number of guests, and in a radio-equipped automobile can bring an entire dinner fifty miles to the lake house for the Johnson party, keeping in touch all the way.

Lyndon Johnson started his motorboat period with an open runabout. He wanted a craft that would carry more people and more refreshments. His staff found a commodious and swift cabin cruiser that is now the "flagship" of the LBJ Texas fleet. One of them remembers the day it was delivered by truck to the lakefront, and put in the water. The maker's representatives started telling Mr. Johnson in detail the features of the new boat. Johnson cut him short:

"How do you start it and where is the throttle?"

His Secret Service guards bought a jet boat so they could keep up with the then Vice President as he cruised up and down the lake. Johnson was exuberant when he discovered that his cruiser would outrun the Secret Service craft. He would race ahead, then joke with the agents on the radio phone asking what made them so slow.

Before he became President, Lyndon Johnson found many occasions to stop in at the LBJ en route to or from his constant succession of speaking engagements. He usually managed things so that there were friends to visit in leisurely conversations aboard his boat, or before the fireplace at the LBJ, or in jouncing rides across the pastures. Mr. and Mrs. Johnson have made a lifelong effort to gather congenial people for interesting evenings. Sometimes Mr. Johnson leads the talking, but often he'll lie back in an easy chair and listen, putting in a question merely to stimulate the guests' accounts of their travels or exposition of their ideas.

The relaxed Lyndon Johnson is still the questing, inventive, preoccupied person who spends every waking moment on ideas for action of every variety—official, business, personal, or plain fun.

He sometimes uses the schoolteacher idiom in half-joking running comment on something a staff aide may be doing, for instance driving him around the ranch: "I'll give you an A on missing that rock . . . B plus on that turn . . . A plus . . . A minus. . . ."

One autumn day in the late 1950's, Johnson had as guest at the ranch a columnist on a nationally circulated newspaper. He took the visitor in an old open-top runabout car he drove in those days, ostensibly to look at the cattle and hunt doves. But Johnson's conversation soon went deeply into a piece of State strategy he had pulled off the week before. As they bounced through the pastures, he went on with the involved story of how he had produced a certain voting result. Occasionally a dove or two flew in range. Johnson lifted his shotgun, fired, kept on talking. If he killed a dove, a companion picked it up. If he missed, he made no comment—he merely continued with his monologue on the Senate.

Lyndon Johnson regretted losing Mary Margaret Wiley, who left his staff to become Mrs. Jack Valenti of Houston. He called her the best secretary he'd ever employed. The relationship between the Johnsons and the Valentis is a close, warm one. Mr. Johnson's staff knew he was awaiting with eager interest the news that Mrs. Valenti had borne her first child. The day of the baby's arrival, a secretary waiting for Mr. Johnson at the LBJ Ranch received the call from Houston. She relayed the word by radio telephone to Johnson, who was en route in the LBJ plane to Austin. "The baby is a little girl, named Courtenay Lynda," said the secretary.

Johnson called for the ranch foreman to come on the radio hookup.

"Didn't we have a heifer calf born today?" he asked.

"Yes, we did."

"Fix up the registration papers on that calf. Show the owner's name as Courtenay Lynda Valenti," he said.

The LBJ cattle herd, started with a few animals, now includes nearly three hundred head. "I never have sold one," said Mr. Johnson recently. "My tax man says I'd better start selling some of them." He is proud of the show animals selected and groomed by his foreman. The show herd has won blue ribbons at several South Texas Hereford exhibitions. Their excellence is merely another evidence that Lyndon Johnson wants to be first, or "A plus," in everything.

Lyndon Johnson's method of getting things done begins most

frequently with a process of trying out ideas and courses of action on one or usually several of the persons he knows best and trusts the most.

Quite often, he has already decided the point, but the decision is tentative until he has tested the situation in conversation. This may be a face-to-face conversation but it is more likely to be a telephone dialogue.

As one friend of the President recently described this screening procedure, it goes this way:

"Let's say a problem comes up. He does a lot of telephoning and he calls, let's say, Jim Rowe, Tommy Corcoran, Clark Clifford, Abe Fortas and Dean Acheson. Now he has a picture in his mind of each man—the picture may not necessarily be correct in all its details, but he has one. He may think to himself, 'OK, there's Rowe, a Northern liberal, a pessimist, and so forth. There's Corcoran, more conservative, an optimist, a little cynical. And he goes right down the line.

"He has a pretty good idea of what each of these men will say on the problem. I don't think he pays a great deal of attention unless one of them says something unexpected. Then he sees a signal he hadn't seen before. I've seen him do it over and over. He's looking for those warning lights."

Another friend verifies the purpose behind Lyndon Johnson's well-known monologues: "He uses his friends as sounding boards, letting his thoughts come out and bounce off them. He doesn't put things down on paper, pro and con, like a lawyer. He talks things out. The chief function of his friends is to let him talk."

Mrs. Johnson is one who not only is a sounding board, but whose responses have great weight with Lyndon Johnson. She is thorough in searching out facts. Her judgment is keen and solid. "If Lady Bird is against something," says one of the family friends, "you'll have an awfully hard time selling it to Lyndon."

The coterie of old friends mentioned above—Abe Fortas, Clark Clifford, Dean Acheson, James Rowe, Tommy Corcoran —became acquainted with Lyndon Johnson when he caught Franklin Roosevelt's fancy by winning his first congressional race in 1937 under the FDR banner. "Take care of that boy," Roosevelt told Corcoran.

Another favorite target of Johnson's questing conversations, and one who is much more than a sounding board indeed, is Robert McNamara. The Secretary of Defense won Johnson's admiration when Johnson sat in Mr. Kennedy's Cabinet. A Johnson description of McNamara at that time is memorable: "There was a tough situation in Europe and McNamara flew over to see what it amounted to. The President called a cabinet meeting to consider the thing one morning. McNamara had to fly all night from Paris to attend the meeting.

"He walked in, this pale, slim fellow with Stacomb on his hair and those school-teacher-looking glasses. You'd think he'd just come from home. He had four experts with him.

"He made his report, at the President's request, and he had every fact and every item and every bit of that business at his fingertips. He never once asked his experts to verify or supplement a thing. I never saw such a fellow."

The President consults McNamara about many matters, industrial and economic, as well as those pertaining more directly to the huge Department of Defense.

Another of the Kennedy appointees admired and trusted by Mr. Johnson is his Secretary of State, Dean Rusk. Those two, along with McGeorge Bundy, are the most influential of all his official family with the President in the conduct of international affairs.

The White House staff itself has become an object of much interest to observers of the Johnson presidency. Its evolution through the spring of 1965 was product of many events.

With Lyndon Johnson as he accompanied John F. Kennedy on the ill-fated tour of Texas in November of 1963 was Jack Valenti, young and successful advertising agency head from Houston. Valenti had met and admired Johnson during Democratic campaigns, had met and married Johnson's favorite secretary, Mary Margaret Wiley, and was in charge, on that star-crossed Kennedy trip, of the promotion and press relations.

After the assassination, and as Lyndon Johnson reached the presidential airplane to be sworn into office, he sent for Valenti. The young man flew back to Washington with the Johnson party, returned home 24 hours later to pick up some clothing, flew back to Washington and has been back in the White House ever since. "He never told me to leave, so I stayed," Valenti says.

Cliff Carter had just worked out an arrangement with Lyndon Johnson not long before November 22, 1963, to operate an office for the Vice President in Austin, Texas, so that his wife and five children could live there. This happy idea was a result of the assassination. Carter was drafted back to Washington at once by the new President.

Bill Moyers, who had been on Johnson's staff before becoming deputy to Sargent Shriver in the Peace Corps, likewise was ordered to the White House on the evening of November 22 and is still there.

Moyers worked for the LBJ broadcasting enterprise while taking a degree in journalism, with honors, from the University of Texas. He went on to Edinburgh University, Scotland, for a year and then attended Southwestern Baptist Theological Seminary at Fort Worth. He is an ordained Baptist minister though he has never held a fulltime pastorate.

The thing that caused him to turn to government instead of a career in the ministry, Moyers said, was a quotation from Thomas Jefferson: "The care of human life and happiness . . . is the first and only legitimate object of good government."

Today that quotation is framed over Moyers' desk as he shepherds for Lyndon Johnson the burgeoning details of the Great Society program.

Horace Busby had been associated with Lyndon Johnson since 1948, had been in Washington for some time publishing a businessman's newsletter and doing public relations work. He, too, got the call after the assassination and soon went on the White House payroll.

George Reedy had been with Mr. Johnson since 1951 as a press aide, speechwriter and researcher. He moved from his hideway in the basement of the capitol to become a member of the White House press staff almost at once after the assassination. When Pierre Salinger resigned suddenly to seek political office in California, Reedy stepped into the position of presidential press secretary.

Until after the 1964 election, Kenneth O'Donnell remained as a key man on the White House staff, working closely with Cliff Carter, who was the Johnson man at the top of the Democratic National Committee. O'Donnell left to help write an account of his years with John Kennedy.

The tragic departure of Walter Jenkins, who had been the top man of the whole Johnson aide structure, put Moyers in the number one position but it was months before the gap was brought under control. Jenkins' vast background knowledge was irreplaceable.

After the 1964 election, Mr. Johnson persuaded Marvin Watson of Texas to join the White House staff. He is, said Johnson, "as wise as my father, as gentle as my mother . . . loyal as another East Texan I know, Lady Bird."

Kermit Gordon, director of the budget, is another close associate of the President, high in his esteem.

There are others, all picked for talent and an ability to work long, hard hours productively and anonymously and tirelessly. The compartmentation is mostly for payroll purposes. "There's no need for an organization chart for men who understand

151

each other," one of them said. They can, and do, handle a multiplicity of work.

One of their chief products in 1965 was the series of special messages from Lyndon Johnson to Congress. Of these, Eric Sevareid recently wrote:

". . . As a reporter who has read more presidential messages than he cares to remember, I can only testify that I have found these documents (from Johnson's desk) on education, on poverty, on the economic state of the union, on conservation, to be superbly conceived, argued with cogency and clothed in language that is always clear and often shining.

"I am sure many minds have worked on them and that some of these minds exist amongst his unofficial kitchen cabinet; no matter, the net result is presidential policy making and policy expression of a very high order, not inferior to those of the Kennedy period and superior to those of the Eisenhower period. Mediocre minds could not possibly have produced these messages, because mediocre men do not recognize or appeal to the highest instincts of the people, as these messages consistently do."

Valenti, a few weeks after he had begun work at the White House, said of his job succinctly: "It demands total excellence, nothing less."

Lyndon Johnson's far-famed reputation as a perfectionist is bearing fruit.

It is this ceaseless urge for perfection, and in politics, for victory, that has caused him to be regarded by rivals as "power mad" or "domineering." Yet he has no capacity for bearing enmities or nursing grudges. A considerable number of former political opponents now regards him as a friend. Usually, Johnson goes more than halfway to patch up their differences.

One commentator examining the Johnson personality at close range has written:

"His idea of politics is like the idea of manliness; if you can't take it, stay home with the women. The result is politics as dazing and unrelenting as a Gulf wind."

Lyndon Johnson's schooling in the rough-and-tumble of Texas politics dated from the days when he listened to oratorical invective as delivered from the stump by such masters as farmer Jim Ferguson and Dan Moody. It is remarkable that Johnson came through this schooling without picking up the habit of invective, but with a full share of the colorful and flamboyant touches for which Texas candidates long have been famous.

Johnson's performances on the platforms and courthouse

lawns have always featured the themes that tend to unify rather than divide the voters: progress, prosperity and peace. He had no taste, and has none today, for the type of political fire-eating so popular a generation ago in Texas. Many an old-timer can still remember the sight and sound of Jim Ferguson leaning forward at the edge of a platform, pulling up the sleeves of his alpaca coat with exaggerated gestures, and trumpeting, "Now don't you good folks on the front row get too close. Tonight we're gonna skin a skunk."

That isn't the kind of force Lyndon Johnson applies to politics. He's a salesman.

One evening, Lyndon Johnson and a few friends sat watching a televised speech by a fellow Texan who had never been friendly to Johnson. After the speech ended, Johnson asked his friends, one at a time, how each one would grade the speech. They put a low rating on it—C or D—thinking this would please him. He set his lips firmly and said, "I'll have to give him an A."

He respects opponents so long as they are fair and straightforward. He has harsh terms for demagogues, and he resents what he calls "mean, vicious, smearing" attacks on his person and his position. As intensely as he plays politics to win, he seems able to judge opponents with a certain objectivity, giving them credit when they show talent, spunk and finesse, and admiring their strong points.

Lyndon Johnson has ingrained respect for political offices, from the presidency to the local constable. As Congressman and Senator, he looked upon the position of President, and the separation of executive from legislative prerogatives, with careful correctness. He could be as partisan as any Democrat but he refused to cross over the line between Congress and the White House in spite of his own tremendous powers in the Senate.

Whatever the future holds for President Lyndon Johnson in the stresses of the world's most demanding position of responsibility, at the most complex stage of world history, those who have known him over the years are sure of this: He will give to the nation the best talent and dedication he is capable of. In the context of his public record, Lyndon Johnson's best very well may be second to none.

APPENDIX

On Memorial Day, 1963, Lyndon B. Johnson, then Vice President of the United States, and Chairman of the President's Committee on Equal Employment Opportunity, spoke at Gettysburg, Pennsylvania, where President Lincoln delivered his immortal Gettysburg Address 100 years before.

On this hallowed ground, heroic deeds were performed and eloquent words were spoken a century ago.

We, the living, have not forgotten—and the world will never forget—the deeds or the words of Gettysburg. We honor them now as we join on this Memorial Day of 1963 in a prayer for permanent peace of the world and fulfillment of our hopes for universal freedom and justice.

We are called to honor our own words of reverent prayer with resolution in the deeds we must perform to preserve peace and the hope of freedom.

We keep a vigil of peace around the world.

Until the world knows no aggressors, until the arms of tyranny have been laid down, until freedom has risen up in every land, we shall maintain our vigil to make sure our sons who died on foreign fields shall not have died in vain.

As we maintain the vigil of peace, we must remember that justice is a vigil, too—a vigil we must keep in our own streets and schools and among the lives of all our people—so that those who died here on their native soil shall not have died in vain.

One hundred years ago, the slave was freed.

One hundred years later, the Negro remains in bondage to the color of his skin.

The Negro today asks justice.

We do not answer him—we do not answer those who lie beneath this soil—when we reply to the Negro by asking, "Patience."

It is empty to plead that the solution to the dilemmas of the present rests on the hands of the clock. The solution is in our hands. Unless we are willing to yield up our destiny of greatness among the civilizations of history, Americans—white and Negro together—must be about the business of resolving the challenge which confronts us now.

Our nation found its soul in honor on these fields of Gettysburg one hundred years ago. We must not lose that soul in dishonor now on the fields of hate.

To ask for patience from the Negro is to ask him to give more of what he has already given enough. But to fail to ask of him—and of all Americans—perseverance within the processes of a free and responsible society would be to fail to ask what the national interest requires of all its citizens.

The law cannot save those who deny it, but neither can the law serve any who do not use it. The history of injustice and inequality is a history of disuse of the law. Law has not failed —and is not failing. We as a nation have failed ourselves by not trusting the law and by not using the law to gain sooner the ends of justice which law alone serves.

If the white over-estimates what he has done for the Negro without the law, the Negro may under-estimate what he is doing and can do for himself with the law.

If it is empty to ask Negro or white for patience, it is not empty—it is merely honest—to ask perseverance. Men may build barricades—and others may hurl themselves against those barricades—but what would happen at the barricades would yield no answers. The answers will only be wrought by our perseverance together. It is deceit to promise more as it would be cowardice to demand less.

In this hour, it is not our respective races which are at stake —it is our nation. Let those who care for their country come forward, North and South, white and Negro, to lead the way through this moment of challenge and decision.

The Negro says, "Now." Others say, "Never." The voice of responsible Americans—the voice of those who died here and the great man who spoke here—their voices say, "Together." There is no other way.

Until Justice is blind to color, until education is unaware of race, until opportunity is unconcerned with the color of men's skins, emancipation will be a proclamation but not a fact. To the extent that the proclamation of emancipation is not fulfilled in fact, to that extent we shall have fallen short of assuring freedom to the free.

*Address by the President before
a joint session of the Congress,
November 27, 1963.*

Mr. Speaker, Mr. President, Members of the House and Senate, my fellow Amercans:

All I have I would have given gladly not to be standing here today.

The greatest leader of our time has been struck down by the foulest deed of our time. Today John Fitzgerald Kennedy lives on in the immortal words and works he left behind. He lives on in the mind and memories of mankind. He lives on in the hearts of his countrymen.

No words are sad enough to express our sense of loss. No words are strong enough to express our determination to continue the forward thrust of America that he began.

The dream of conquering the vastness of space—the dream of partnership across the Atlantic—and across the Pacific as well—the dream of a Peace Corps in less developed lands—the dream of education for our youth—the dream of jobs for all who seek them—the dream of care for our elderly—the dream of an all-out attack on mental illness—and above all, the dream of equal rights for all Americans, whatever their race or color—these and other American dreams have been vitalized by his drive and dedication.

Now the ideas and ideals which he so nobly represented must and will be translated into effective action.

Under John Kennedy's leadership, this Nation has demonstrated that it has the courage to seek peace, and the fortitude to risk war. We have proved that we are a good and reliable friend to those who seek peace and freedom. We have shown that we can also be a formidable foe to those who reject the path of peace and who seek to impose upon us or our allies the yoke of tyranny.

This Nation will keep its commitments from South Vietnam to West Berlin. We will be unceasing in the search for peace; resourceful in our pursuit of areas of agreement even with those with whom we differ; and generous and loyal to those who join with us in common cause.

In this age where there can be no losers in peace and no victors in war—we must recognize the obligation to match national strength with national restraint—we must be prepared at one and the same time for both the confrontation of power and the limitation of power—we must be ready to defend the national interest and to negotiate the common interest. This is the path that we shall continue to pursue. Those who test our courage will find it strong and those who seek our friendship will find it honorable. We will demonstrate anew that the strong can be just in the use of strength—and the just can be strong in the defense of justice.

We will carry on the fight against poverty and misery, ignorance and disease—in other lands and in our own.

We will serve all of the Nation, not one section or one sector, or one group, but all Americans. These are the United States—a united people with unity of purpose.

Our American unity does not depend upon unanimity. We have differences; but now, as in the past, we can derive from those differences strength, not weakness; wisdom, not despair. Both as a people and as a government we can unite upon a program which is wise, just and constructive.

For 32 years, Capitol Hill has been my home. I have shared many moments of pride with you—pride in the ability of the Congress of the United States to act; to meet any crisis; to distill from our differences strong programs of national action.

An assassin's bullet has thrust upon me the awesome burden of the Presidency. I am here today to say that I need your help; I cannot bear this burden alone. I need the help of all Americans. This Nation has experienced a profound shock and in this critical moment it is our duty—yours and mine— as the Government of the United States—to do away with uncertainty and to show that we are capable of decisive action —that from the brutal loss of our leader we will derive not weakness but strength—that we can and will act and act now.

From the chamber of representative government let all the world know, and none misunderstand, that I rededicate this Government to the unswerving support of the United Nations —to the honorable and determined execution of our commitments to our allies—to the maintenance of military strength second to none—to the expansion of our foreign trade—to the re-enforcement of our programs of mutual assistance and cooperation in Asia and Africa—and to our Alliance for Progress in this hemisphere.

On the 20th of January, in 1961, John F. Kennedy told his countrymen that our national work would not be finished "in the first one thousand days, nor in the life of this administration, nor even perhaps in our lifetime on this planet. But"— he said—"let us begin."

Today in this moment of new resolve, I would say to my fellow Americans, Let Us Continue.

This is our challenge—not to hesitate, not to pause, not to turn about and linger over this evil moment but to continue on our course so that we may fulfill the destiny history has set for us. Our most immediate tasks are here on this Hill.

First, no memorial oration or eulogy could more eloquently honor President Kennedy's memory than the earliest possible passage of the Civil Rights bill for which he fought. We have talked long enough in this country about equal rights. We have talked for 100 years or more. Yes, it is time now to write the next chapter—and to write it in books of law.

I urge you again, as I did in 1957, and again in 1960, to enact a civil rights law so that we can move forward to eliminate from this nation every trace of discrimination and oppression based upon race or color. There could be no greater source of strength to this nation both at home and abroad.

And second, no act of ours could more fittingly continue the work of President Kennedy than the earliest passage of the Tax bill for which he fought—a bill designed to increase our national income, our Federal revenues, and our insurance against recession. That bill, if passed without delay, means more security for those now working and more jobs for those now without them.

In short, this is no time for delay. It is a time for action—strong, forward-looking action on the pending education bills to help bring the light of learning to every home and hamlet in America—strong, forward-looking action on youth employment opportunities, strong forward-looking action on the pending foreign aid bill, making clear that we are not forfeiting our responsibilities to this Hemisphere or to the world, nor erasing executive flexibility in the conduct of foreign affairs—and strong, forward-looking action on the remaining appropriation bills.

In this new spirit of action the Congress can expect the full cooperation and support of the Executive Branch. And in particular I pledge that the expenditures of the Government will be administered with the utmost thrift and frugality. I will insist that the Government get a dollar's value for a dollar spent. The Government will set an example of prudence and economy. This does not mean we will not meet our unfilled needs or that we will not honor our commitments. We will do both.

As one who has long served in both Houses of the Congress, I firmly believe in the independence and integrity of the Legislative Branch. I promise you that I shall always respect this.

It is deep in the marrow of my bones. With equal firmness, I believe in the capacity and the ability of the Congress, despite the divisions of opinion which characterize our nation, to act —to act wisely, vigorously and speedily when the need arises.

The need is here. The need is now. I ask your help.

I know we meet in grief; but let us also meet in renewed dedication and renewed vigor. Let us meet in action, in tolerance and mutual understanding.

John Kennedy's death commands what his life conveyed— that America must move forward. The time has come for Americans of all races and creeds and political beliefs to understand and respect one another. Let us put an end to the teaching and preaching of hate and evil and violence. Let us turn away from the fanatics of the far left and the far right, from the apostles of bitterness and bigotry, from those defiant of law, and those who pour venom into our nation's bloodstream.

I profoundly hope that the tragedy and torment of these terrible days will bind us together in new fellowship, making us one people in our sorrow. Let us here highly resolve that John Fitzgerald Kennedy did not live—or die—in vain. And on this Thanksgiving eve, as we gather together to ask the Lord's blessing, let us unite in those familiar and cherished words:

> *"America, America,*
> *God shed His grace on thee,*
> *And crown thy good*
> *With brotherhood*
> *From sea to shining sea."*

Following is the text of President Johnson's personal Thanksgiving Day message to the American people. The speech was delivered over nationwide television and radio networks on November 28, 1963.

My fellow Americans: On yesterday, I went before the Congress to speak for the first time as President of the United States.

Tonight, on this Thanksgiving, I come before you to ask your help, to ask your strength, to ask your prayers that God may guard this republic and guide my every labor.

All of us have lived through seven days that none of us will ever forget. We are not given the divine wisdom to answer why this has been, but we are given the human duty of determining what is to be, what is to be for America, for the world, for the cause we lead, for all the hopes that live in our hearts.

A great leader is dead; a great nation must move on. Yesterday is not ours to recover, but tomorrow is ours to win or to lose. I am resolved that we shall win the tomorrows before us. So I ask you to join me in that resolve, determined that from this midnight of tragedy, we shall move toward a new American greatness.

More than any generation before us, we have cause to be thankful on this Thanksgiving Day. Our harvests are bountiful, our factories flourish, our homes are safe, our defenses are secure.

We live in peace. The goodwill of the world pours out for us, but more than these blessings, we know tonight that our system is strong, strong and secure. A deed that was meant to tear us apart has bound us together. Our system has passed. You have passed a great test. You have shown what John F. Kennedy called upon us to show in his proclamation of this Thanksgiving: That decency of purpose, that steadfastness of resolve and that strength of will which we inherit from our forefathers.

What better conveys what is best for America than this. On Saturday when these great burdens had been mine only hours, the first two citizens to call upon me and to offer their whole support were Dwight D. Eisenhower and Harry S. Truman.

Since last Friday, Americans have turned to the good, to the decent values of our life. These have served us. Yes, these have saved us. The service of our public institution and our public men is the salvation of us all from the Supreme Court to the states. And how much better would it be? How much more sane it would be, how much more decent and American it would be if all Americans could spend their fortunes and could give their time and spend their energies helping our system and its servants to solve your problems instead of pouring out the venom and the hate that stalemate us in progress.

I have served in Washington 32 years—32 years yesterday. I have seen five presidents fill this awesome office. I have known them well and I have counted them all as friends: President Herbert Hoover, President Franklin Roosevelt, President Harry Truman, President Dwight Eisenhower, and President John Kennedy.

In each administration, the greatest burden that the President had to bear had been the burden of his own countrymen's unthinking and unreasoning hate and division. So, in these days, the fate of this office is the fate of us all. I would ask all Americans on this day of prayer and reverence to think on these things. Let all who speak and all who teach and all who preach and all who publish and all who broadcast and all who read or listen—let them reflect upon their responsibilities to bind our wounds, to heal our sores, to make our society well and whole for the tasks ahead of us. It is this work that I most wanted us to do, to banish rancor from our words and malice from our hearts, to close down the poison spring of hatred and intolerance and fanaticism; to protect our unity north and south, east and west; to hasten the day when bias of race, religion and region is no more; and to make the day when our great energies and decencies and spirit will be free of the burdens that we have borne too long.

Our view is outward. Our thrust is forward, but we remember in our hearts this brave young man who lives in honored eternal rest across the Potomac. We remember him; we remember his wonderful and courageous widow that we all love. We remember Caroline and John and all the great family who gave the nation this son and brother.

And to honor his memory and the future of the works he started, I have today determined that Station No. 1 of the Atlantic missile range and a NASA launch operation center in Florida shall hereafter be known as the John F. Kennedy Space Center.

I have also acted today with the understanding and the support of my friend, the governor of Florida, Farris Bryant, to change the name of Cape Canaveral. It shall be known hereafter as Cape Kennedy.

On this Thanksgiving Day, as we gather in the warmth of our families, in the mutual love and respect that we have for one another, and as we bow our heads in submission to Divine Providence, let us also thank God for the years that he gave us inspiration through his servant, John F. Kennedy.

Let us today renew our dedication to the ideals that are American. Let us pray for his divine wisdom in banishing from our land any injustice or intolerance or oppression to any of our fellow Americans, whatever their opinion, whatever the color of their skins—for God made all of us, not some of us, in his image. All of us, not just some of us, are his children.

And, finally, to you as your President, I ask that you remember your country and remember me each day in your prayers, and I pledge to you the best within me to work for a new American greatness, a new day when peace is more secure, when justice is more universal, when freedom is more strong in every home of all mankind.

Address by the President on the occasion of his Inauguration, January 20, 1965.

My fellow countrymen: On this occasion, the oath I have taken before you—and before God—is not mine alone, but ours together. We are one nation and one people. Our fate as a nation and our future as a people rests not upon one citizen but upon all citizens. That is the majesty and the meaning of this moment.

For every generation, there is a destiny. For some, history decides. For this generation, the choice must be our own.

Even now, a rocket moves toward Mars. It reminds us that the world will not be the same for our children, or even ourselves in a short span of years. The next man to stand here will look out on a scene that is different from our own, because ours is a time of change—rapid and fantastic change, baring the secrets of nature, multiplying the nations, placing in uncertain hands new weapons for mastery and destruction, shaking old values and uprooting old ways.

Our destiny in the midst of change will rest on the unchanged character of our people, and on their faith.

They came here—the exile and the stranger, brave but frightened—to find a place where a man could be his own man.

They made a covenant with this land. Conceived in justice, written in liberty, bound in union, it was meant one day to inspire the hopes of all mankind, and it binds us still. If we keep its terms, we shall flourish.

First, justice was the promise that all who made the journey would share in the fruits of the land.

In a land of great wealth, families must not live in hopeless poverty. In a land rich in harvest, children just must not go hungry. In a land of healing miracles, neighbors must not suffer and die untended. In a great land of learning and scholars, young people must be taught to read and write.

For more than 30 years that I have served this nation, I have believed that this injustice to our people—this waste of our resources—was our real enemy. For 30 years or more,

162

with the resources I have had, I have vigilantly fought against it. I have learned, and I know that it will not surrender easily.

But change has given us new weapons. Before this generation of Americans is finished, this enemy will not only retreat —it will be conquered.

Justice requires us to remember—when any citizen denies his fellow, saying, "His color is not mine," or "His beliefs are strange and different"—in that moment he betrays America, though his forebears created this nation.

Liberty was the second article of our covenant. It was self-government. It was our Bill of Rights. But it was more. America would be a place where each man could be proud to be himself—stretching his talents, rejoicing in his work, important in the life of his neighbors and his nation.

This has become more difficult in a world where change and growth seem to tower beyond the control, and even the judgment, of men. We must work to provide the knowledge and the surroundings which can enlarge the possibilities of every citizen.

The American covenant called on us to help show the way for the liberation of man. And that is today our goal. Thus, if as a nation there is much outside our control, as a people no stranger is outside our hope.

Change has brought new meaning to that old mission. We can never again stand aside prideful in isolation. Terrific dangers and troubles that we once called "foreign" now constantly live among us. If American lives must end, and American treasure be spilled, in countries that we barely know, then that is the price that change has demanded of conviction and of our enduring covenant.

Think of our world as it looks from that rocket that's heading toward Mars. It is like a child's globe, hanging in space, the continents stuck to its side like colored maps. We are all fellow passengers on a dot of earth. And each of us, in the span of time, has really only a moment among our companions.

How incredible it is that in this fragile existence we should hate and destroy one another. There are possibilities enough for all who will abandon mastery over others to pursue mastery over nature. There is world enough for all to seek their happiness in their own way.

And our nation's course is abundantly clear. We aspire to nothing that belongs to others. We seek no dominion over our fellow man, but man's dominion over tyranny and misery.

But more is required. Men want to be part of a common enterprise—a cause greater than themselves. And each of

163

us must find a way to advance the purpose of the nation, and thus find new purpose for ourselves. Without this, we will simply become a nation of strangers.

The third article is union. To those who were small and few against the wilderness, the success of liberty demanded the strength of the Union. Two centuries of change have made this true again.

No longer need capitalist and worker, farmer and clerk, city and countryside, struggle to divide our bounty. By working shoulder to shoulder together we can increase the bounty of all.

We have discovered that every child who learns, and every man who finds work, and every sick body that's made whole— like a candle added to an altar—brightens the hope of all the faithful.

So let us reject any among us who seek to reopen old wounds and rekindle old hatreds. They stand in the way of a seeking nation.

Let us now join reason to faith, and action to experience, to transform our unity of interest into a unity of purpose. For the hour and the day and the time are here to achieve progress without strife, to achieve change without hatred; not without difference of opinion, but without the deep and abiding divisions which scar the Union for generations.

Under this covenant of justice, liberty and union, we have become a nation; prosperous, great and mighty. And we have kept our freedom.

But we have no promise from God that our greatness will endure. We have been allowed by Him to seek greatness with the sweat of our hands and the strength of our spirit.

I do not believe that the Great Society is the ordered, changeless and sterile battalion of the ants.

It is the excitement of becoming—always becoming, trying, probing, falling, resting and trying again—but always trying and always gaining.

In each generation—with toil and tears—we have had to earn our heritage again.

If we fail now, then we will have forgotten in abundance what we learned in hardship: that democracy rests on faith, that freedom asks more than it gives and the judgment of God is harshest on those who are most favored.

If we succeed, it will not be because of what we have, but it will be because of what we are; not because of what we own, but rather because of what we believe.

For we are a nation of believers. Underneath the clamor of building and the rush of our day's pursuits, we are believers in justice and liberty and union, and in our own Union. We believe that every man must some day be free. And we believe in ourselves.

And that is the mistake that our enemies have always made. In my lifetime—in depression and in war—they have awaited our defeat. Each time, from the secret places of the American heart, came forth the faith that they could not see or that they could not even imagine. It brought us victory. And it will again.

For this is what America is all about. It is the uncrossed desert and the unclimbed ridge. It is the star that is not reached and the harvest that's sleeping in the unplowed ground.

Is our world gone? We say farewell. Is a new world coming? We welcome it—and we will bend it to the hopes of man.

And to those trusted public servants and to my family and those close friends of mine who have followed me down a long winding road and to all the people of this Union and the world I will repeat today what I said on that sorrowful day in November last year [1963]: I will lead and I will do the best I can.

But you—you must look within your own hearts to the old promises and to the old dream. They will lead you best of all.

For myself, I ask only in the words of an ancient leader: "Give me now wisdom and knowledge, that I may go out and come in before this people: for who can judge this thy people, that is so great?"

Address by the President before a joint session of the Congress, March 15, 1965.

Mr. President, Mr. Speaker, members of the Congress, my fellow Americans:

I speak tonight for the dignity of man and the destiny of democracy.

I urge members of both parties—Americans of all religions and colors—from every section—to join me in that cause.

At times, history and fate meet at a single time in a single place to shape a turning point in man's unending search for freedom. So it was at Lexington and Concord. So it was a century ago at Appamatox. So it was last week in Selma, Ala.

There, long-suffering men and women peacefully protested

the denial of their rights as Americans. Many were brutally assaulted. One good man—a man of God—was killed.

There is no cause for pride in what happened in Selma.

There is no cause for self-satisfaction in the long denial of equal rights of millions of Americans.

But there is cause for hope and for fate in our democracy in what is happening here tonight.

For the cries of pain, the hymns and protests of oppressed people, have summoned into convocation all the majesty of the government of the greatest nation on earth.

Our mission is at once the oldest and most basic of this country: To right wrong, to do justice, to serve man.

In our time we have come to live with moments of great crisis. Our lives have been marked with debate about great issues—issues of war and peace of prosperity and depression.

But rarely, in any time, does an issue lay bare the secret heart of America itself.

Rarely are we met with a challenge, not to our growth or abundance, our welfare or security—but to the values and the purpose and meaning of our nation.

The issue of equal rights for American Negroes is such an issue. And should we defeat every enemy, double our wealth, conquer the stars and still be unequal to this issue, then we will have failed as a people and a nation.

For with a country as with a person, "what is a man profited, if he shall gain the whole world, and lose his own soul?"

There is no Negro problem. There is no Southern problem or Northern problem, there is only an American problem.

And we are met as Americans to solve it.

This was the first nation in the history of the world to be founded with a purpose. The great phrases of that purpose still found in every American heart, North and South: "All men are created equal"—"Government by consent of the governed"—"Give me liberty or give me death." Those are not just clever words or empty theories.

In their name, Americans have fought and died for two centuries and today are risking their lives.

Those words are a promise to every citizen that he shall share in the dignity of man. This dignity cannot be found in a man's possessions or his power or his position.

It rests on his right to be treated as a man equal in opportunity to all others. It says that he shall share in freedom, choose his leaders, educate his children, provide for his family according to his ability and merits as a human being.

To apply to any other test—to deny a man his hopes because of his color or race, his religion or the place of his birth

—is not only to do injustice, it is to deny America and to dishonor the dead who gave their lives for freedom.

Our fathers believed that if this noble view of the rights of man was to flourish, it must be rooted in democracy. The most basic right of all was the right to choose your own leaders. The history of this country is, in large measure, the history of the expansion of that right to all our people.

Many of the issues of civil rights are complex and difficult. But above this there can be no argument. Every American citizen must have an equal right to vote.

There is no reason which can excuse the denial of that right. There is no duty which weighs more heavily on us than the duty to insure that right.

Yet, the harsh fact is that in many places in this country men and women are kept from voting because they are Negroes.

Every device of which human ingenuity is capable has been used to deny this right. The Negro citizen may go to register only to be told that the day is wrong, the hour is late, or the official in charge is absent.

If he persists, and manages to present himself to the registrar, he may be disqualified because he did not spell out his middle name or because he abbreviated a word on the application.

If he manages to fill out an application he is given a test. The registrar is the sole judge of whether he passes this test.

He may be asked to recite the entire Constitution, or explain the most complex provisions of state law. Even a college degree cannot be used to prove that he can read or write.

For the fact is that the only way to pass these barriers is to show a white skin.

Experience has clearly shown that the existing process of law cannot overcome systematic and ingenious discrimination.

No law we now have on the books can insure the right to vote when local officials are determined to deny it.

In such a case our duty is clear. The Constitution says no person shall be kept from voting because of his race or color. We have all sworn an oath before God to support and defend that Constitution. We must now act in obedience to that oath.

Wednesday, I will send to Congress a law designed to eliminate illegal barriers to the right to vote.

This bill will strike down restrictions to voting in all elections—federal, state and local—which have been used to deny Negroes the right to vote.

It will establish a simple, uniform standard which cannot

167

be used however ingenious the effort to flout our Constitution.

It will provide for citizens to be registered by officials of the United States government if state officials refuse to co-operate.

It will eliminate tedious, unnecessary lawsuits which delay the right to vote.

Finally, this legislation will ensure that properly registered individuals are not prohibited from voting.

I will welcome suggestions from the Congress on ways to strengthen this law and make it more effective. But experience has plainly shown that this is the only path to carry out the command of the Constitution.

To those who seek to avoid action by their national government in their communities—who seek to maintain purely local control over elections—the answer is simple.

Open your polling places to all your people.

Allow men and women to register and vote whatever the color of their skin.

Extend the rights of citizenship to every citizen.

There is no constitutional issue here. The command of the Constitution is plain.

There is no moral issue. It is wrong to deny any American the right to vote.

There is no issue of states rights or national rights. There is only the struggle for human rights.

I have no doubt what will be your answer.

The last time a President sent a civil rights bill to Congress it contained a provision to protect voting rights. That bill was passed after eight long months of debate.

And when that bill came to my desk for signature the heart of the voting provision had been eliminated.

This time, on this issue, there must be no delay, no hesitation, no compromise with our purpose.

We cannot refuse to protect the right of Americans to vote.

We cannot wait another eight months. We have already waited 100 years and more. The time for waiting is gone.

I ask you to work long hours, nights and week-ends to pass this bill.

For outside this chamber is the outraged conscience of a nation—the grave concern of many nations—and the harsh judgment of history on our acts.

But even if we pass this bill, the battle will not be over. What happened in Selma is part of a far larger movement which reaches into every section and state of America.

It is the effort of American Negroes to secure for themselves the full blessings of American life.

Their cause must be our cause too. It is not just Negroes, but all of us, who must overcome the crippling legacy of bigotry and injustice. And we shall overcome.

As a man whose roots go deeply into Southern soil I know how agonizing racial feelings are. I know how difficult it is to reshape attitudes and the structure of society.

But a century has passed since the Negro was freed. And he is not fully free.

A century has passed since equality was promised. And he is not equal.

A century has passed since the day of promise. And the promise is unkept.

The time of justice has now come. No force can hold it back. It is right—in the eyes of man and God—that it should come. And when it does, that day will brighten the lives of every American.

For Negroes are not the only victims. How many white children have gone uneducated—how many white families have lived in poverty—how many white lives have been scarred by fear because we have wasted our energy and substance to maintain the barriers of hatred and terror.

Those who ask you to hold on to the past do so at the cost of denying you your future.

This great, rich, restless country can offer opportunity and education and hope to all—black and white, North and South, sharecroppers and city dwellers.

These are the enemies—poverty and ignorance—and not our fellow man. And these too shall be overcome.

Let no one, in any section, look with prideful righteousness on the troubles of his neighbors. There is no part of America where the promise of equality has been fully kept.

In Buffalo as well as Birmingham, in Philadelphia as well as Selma, Americans are struggling for the fruits of freedom.

This is one nation. What happens in Selma or in Cincinnati is a matter of legitimate concern to every citizen. But let each of us look within our own communities, and our own hearts, and root out injustice there.

Tonight, men from the South as well as the North, men from the East as well as from the West, are all Americans all fighting together in Viet Nam. Men from every region fought for us across the world 20 years ago.

In these common dangers and these common sacrifices the South made its contribution of honor and gallantry no less than any other region of the great republic.

I have not the slightest doubt that good men from everywhere in this country—from the Great Lakes down to the Gulf of Mexico, from the Golden Gate to the harbors along the Atlantic—will rally now together in this cause to vindicate the freedom of us all.

For all of us owe this duty: All of us will respond to it.

The real hero of this struggle is the American Negro. His actions and protests—his courage to risk safety and even life—have awakened the conscience of the nation.

His demonstrations have been designed to call attention to injustice, to provoke change and stir reform. He has called upon us to make good the promise of America.

And who among us can say we would have made the same progress were it not for his persistent bravery, and his faith in American democracy.

For at the heart of battle for equality is a belief in the democratic process. Equality depends not on the force of arms but the force of moral right—not on recourse to violence but on respect for law.

We intend to fight this battle where it should be fought—in the courts, in the Congress and in the hearts of men.

We must preserve the right of free speech and the right of free assembly. But the right of free speech does not carry with it the right to endanger the safety of others on a public highway.

We do have a right to protest—and a right to march under conditions that do not infringe the constitutional rights of our neighbors. I intend to protect all these rights as long as I am permitted to serve in this office.

We will guard against violence, knowing it strikes from our hands the very weapons with which he seek progress—obedience to law, and belief in American values.

In Selma as elsewhere we seek peace. We seek order. We seek unity.

But we will not accept the peace of stifled rights, the order imposed by fear, the unity that stifles protests. For peace cannot be purchased at the cost of liberty.

In Selma, as in every city, we are working for just and peaceful settlements. We must remember that after this speech—after the police and the marshals have gone—after this bill is passed, the people of Selma must still live and work together.

When the attention of the nation has gone elsewhere, they must try to heal the wounds and build a new community. This cannot easily be done on a battleground of violence as the history of the South itself shows.

It is in recognition of this that men of both races have shown impressive responsibility in recent days.

The bill I am presenting will be known as a civil rights bill. But in a larger sense, most of the program I am recommending is a civil rights program. Its object is to open the city of hope to all of our people.

All Americans must have the right to vote. And we are going to give them that right.

All Americans must have the privileges of citizenship regardless of race. And they are going to have those privileges.

But to exercise that privilege takes more than legal light. It requires a trained mind and a healthy body. It requires a decent home, and the chance to find a job and opportunity to escape from poverty.

Of course people cannot contribute to the nation if they are never taught to read or write, if their bodies are stunted from hunger, if their sickness goes untended, if their life is spent in hopeless poverty.

We want to open the gates to opportunity. But we are also going to give all our people—black and white—the help they need to walk through those gates.

My first job after college was as a teacher in a small Mexican-American school. My students were poor, and often hungry, and they knew even in their youth the pain of prejudice.

They did not understand why people disliked them. But they knew it was so. You could see it in their eyes.

I often walked home after classes wishing there was more I could do. But all I knew was to teach them the little I knew —hoping it might help them against the hardships that lay ahead.

Somehow you never forget what poverty and hatred can do when you see its scars on the hopeful face of a child.

I never thought then that I might be standing here. It never occurred to me that I might have the chance to help the sons of those students—and people like them all over this country.

But now that I have this chance, I mean to take it.

And I hope that you will take it with me.

This is the richest and most powerful country which ever occupied the globe. The might of past empires is little compared to ours.

But I do not want to be the President who built empires, or sought grandeur, or extended dominion.

I want to be the President who educated young children to the wonders of their world—the President who fed the hungry —and helped the poor to find their own way—and enriched the simple, daily lives of every family.

171

And I want to be the President who helped to end hatred among his fellow men, and war among the brothers of this earth.

And I want to share this task with you, and with the people we serve. I want this to be the Congress—Democrats and Republicans alike—which did all these things.

Beyond this great chamber of the people we serve who can tell what deep and unspoken hopes are in their hearts tonight?

We all can guess, from our own lives, how difficult they often find their own pursuit of happiness. They look most of all to themselves for their future. But they also look to us.

Above the pyramid of the Great Seal of the United States it says—in Latin—"He has favored our undertaking."

God will not favor everything we do. It is rather our duty to divine His will. But I cannot help believing He truly favors the undertaking we begin tonight.

OFFICIAL VOTE

WASHINGTON, Dec. 12 (A.P.)—The final popular vote for president, including the state-by-state vote for Johnson, Goldwater and other candidates, and the percentage of the presidential vote each received:

State	Total Vote	Johnson	Pct.	Goldwater	Pct.	Other	Pct.
Ala.	689,817	......	......	479,085	69.5	210,732	30.5
Alaska	67,259	44,329	65.9	22,930	34.1	......	..
Ariz.	480,783	237,765	49.5	242,206	50.4	482	.1
Ark.	2,560,426	314,197	56.1	243,264	43.4	2,965	.5
Cal.	7,050,985	4,171,877	59.2	2,879,108	40.8	......	.5
Colo.	772,749	476,024	61.6	296,725	38.4	......	..
Conn.	1,218,578	826,269	67.8	390,996	32.1	1,313	.1
Del.	201,334	122,704	60.9	78,093	38.8	537	.5
D. C.	198,597	169,796	85.5	28,801	14.5	......	.5
Fla.	1,854,481	948,540	51.1	905,941	48.9	......	..
Ga.	1,139,157	522,557	45.9	616,600	54.1	......	..
Hawaii	207,271	163,249	78.8	44,022	21.2	......	..
Idaho	292,477	148,920	50.9	143,557	49.1	......	..
Ill.	4,702,779	2,796,833	59.5	1,905,946	40.5	......	..
Ind.	2,091,606	1,170,848	56.0	911,118	43.6	9,640	.4
Iowa	1,184,539	733,030	61.9	449,148	37.9	2,361	.2
Kan.	857,901	464,028	54.1	386,579	45.1	7,294	.8
Ky.	1,046,132	669,659	61.0	372,977	35.7	3,496	.3
La.	896,293	387,068	43.2	509,225	56.8	......	..
Maine	380,965	262,264	68.8	118,701	31.2	......	..
Md.	1,116,407	730,912	65.5	385,495	34.5	......	..
Mass.	2,344,798	1,786,422	76.2	549,727	23.4	8,649	.4
Mich.	3,203,102	2,136,615	66.7	1,060,152	33.1	6,335	.2
Minn.	1,554,462	991,117	63.8	559,624	36.0	3,721	.2
Miss.	409,038	52,591	12.9	356,447	87.1	......	..
Mo.	1,817,879	1,164,344	64.0	653,535	36.0	......	..
Mont.	278,628	164,246	58.9	113,032	40.6	1,350	.5
Neb.	584,154	307,307	52.6	276,847	47.4	......	..
Nev.	135,433	79,339	58.6	56,094	41.4	......	..
N. H.	286,094	182,065	63.6	104,029	36.4	......	..
N. J.	2,846,770	1,867,671	61.0	963,843	33.9	15,256	.5
N. M.	327,647	194,017	59.2	131,838	40.2	1,792	.6
N. Y.	7,166,015	4,913,156	68.6	2,243,559	31.3	9,300	.1
N. C.	1,424,983	800,139	56.2	624,844	43.8	......	..
N. D.	258,389	149,784	58.0	108,207	41.9	398	.1
Ohio	3,969,196	2,498,331	62.9	1,470,865	37.1	......	..
Okla.	932,499	519,834	55.7	412,665	44.3	......	..
Ore.	783,796	501,017	63.9	282,779	36.1	......	..
Pa.	4,818,668	3,130,228	65.0	1,672,892	34.7	15,548	.3
R. I.	390,078	315,463	80.9	74,615	19.1	......	..
S. C.	524,748	215,700	41.1	309,048	58.9	......	..
S. D.	293,118	163,010	55.6	130,108	44.4	......	..
Tenn.	1,144,046	635,047	55.5	508,965	44.5	34	..
Tex.	2,626,811	1,633,185	63.3	958,566	36.5	5,060	.2
Utah	400,310	219,628	54.9	180,682	45.1	......	..
Vt.	163,069	108,127	66.3	54,942	33.7	......	..
Va.	1,042,267	558,038	53.5	481,334	46.2	2,895	.3

State	Total Vote	Johnson	Pct.	Goldwater	Pct.	Other	Pct.
Wash.	1,258,374	779,699	62.0	470,366	37.4	8,309	.6
W. Va.	792,040	538,087	67.9	253,953	32.1	......	..
Wis.	1,691,815	1,050,424	62.1	638,495	37.7	2,896	.2
Wyo.	142,716	80,718	56.5	61,998	43.5	......	..
Totals	70,621,479	43,126,218	61.0	27,174,898	38.5	320,363	.5

Notes: — Alabama—No Democratic electors pledged to Johnson were on the ballot. Figures represent vote for highest Republican elector and highest unpledged Democratic elector.

New York — Johnson total includes 342,432 Liberal Party votes.

BILLY GRAHAM

THE MAN WHO WALKS WITH GOD

by Glenn Daniels

An important new biography about one of the great men of God—Billy Graham—the man who put Christ into Christianity for 30 million people.

52-330, 50¢

PORTRAIT OF
PATTON

Harry H. Semmes

A biography of the greatest combat general of
World War II . . . the man called BLOOD AND
GUTS

"Every inch a fighting man." *(Army Times)*

54-701, 75¢
